To Brother D.

Happy Earthday

August 23

Garry Hamilton

Lancing of the
Bullet Wound

from: Garry

Bless

Disclaimer

The contents in this book are offered for informational purposes only and are protected under freedom of speech. I do not give medical advice, nor should the contents be construed as such.

There is nothing in this book that is intended to diagnose or treat any disease, condition, disability, or illness. Before making any changes to your diet, prescribed drug use, way of life, or exercise regime, it is wise to first consult a qualified health professional.

The information within the book is provided within the narrative and the reader must assume all risks from the use, non-use, or misuse of this information. Furthermore, the information is generally not supported by conventional medicine or recognised by individual physicians. It is, however, the truth.

To protect the privacy of the characters mentioned herein, the names of individuals and the locations have been changed.

To my children,
Marcella, Osiris, Omari, Isis, Chione
and my wife, Caroline.

Acknowledgments

So many characters, whose path I have been fortunate to cross along my journey, have played a part in my life, even if sometimes on just a fleeting scale. From the postman to the bus driver, the shopkeeper to the refuse collector, you all deserve your place. My grateful thanks especially to the nurses who genuinely cared about my welfare and who looked after me with such dedication and good spirit.

Foreword

This story surrounds an episode in my life which happened around twenty-one years ago. Its knock-on effects rippled out in a way I could never have predicted. I hope that it will act as a beacon of light for you and your life journey.

It was first published in 2012 when austerity cuts were sweeping the nation, and the poli-tricks propaganda machine was raging heartlessly around the world. The conspiracy theorists intensified their message of a terrifyingly dreadful future. There was no way out. Everything was hopeless. Adding to the general mix of sorrow, we also had indiscriminate scaremongering and misinformation spilling from the mouths of media groups. It didn't help that vulnerable and disabled people had now fallen prey to political demonising and finger pointing, a worthless lot, fair game for picking on.

And here we are ten years later when the masses walk along the street, heads bowed, eyes wide open, staring at a pocket-sized hand-held device…while frequently bumping into a lamppost.

Thumbs and fingers stroke this small, illuminated screen, eagerly searching for something or other of immense importance that requires their all-consuming attention. Friends walk right past each other, disarmingly oblivious to each other's presence, their eyes fixed on their hi-tech, mobile companion. Even the dog gets ignored.

The world has become digitalised, and so too have many of its inhabitants.

However, it is your freedom from doubt, fear, worry, and all the rest of life's turmoil of difficult emotions that is my reason for sharing my short, hopefully potent, story. I want something to resonate with you and remind you that you are not alone.

I may not be able to do very much to change certain habits and the accepted way of doing things today but if this book helps just one human being to realise that they have the internal power to heal so much in a sometimes jumbled up world, by healing themselves, then I will have succeeded.

G.H., 2023

Contents

1

The Café

From the outset of putting pen to paper, I quickly discovered that I was not familiar with the mechanics of writing a story based on a snapshot of time in my life. I wanted to procrastinate, that go-to obstacle whenever we are confronted with something unfamiliar and big to tackle. I will begin somewhere.

My mother was a skilled seamstress and my father a skilled carpenter. My parents were Jamaican migrants, who had come to Britain during the 1950's and 1960's. It was at the time when the British government was looking to its overseas colonies for help; plagued with high labour shortages and with many posts to fill, Britain needed a workforce that would help to rebuild the country after the War. Thousands of fit young men had died. Inviting the migrants from overseas seemed the perfect solution.

I was born in 1963 and David, my siblings, and I grew up in a relatively welcoming and sociable neighbourhood in the city of Bristol, in a district called Montpelier. It was multicultural and generally safe and a friendly part of town. Like most cities there was an unfortunate area that appeared to be a honey pot for police and crime. We grew up on the borders of such an area in Bristol called St. Pauls, separated by one main road.

However, St. Pauls was no less unsociable than anywhere else. I guess it gained its notoriety due to a café situated on the Grosvenor Road that allegedly sold weed on the premises, which it had been doing since the 1960's. It was perhaps a prototype for the cafes of Amsterdam.

St Pauls was one of those areas in a city that for whatever reason couldn't shake off decades of a bad reputation. It had a long history of being demonised by the media and police alike. The neighbourhood was full of people from all walks of life; they were good people, a close-knit community where inhabitants cared about each other. Nonetheless, constant police raids on the café attracted bad publicity and media attention towards this tiny strip of road, thus creating a spectre of fear for people living outside the area, people who knew no different.

Yet that ordinary High Street café stood as a symbol of defiance against the 'Babylon' of social injustice and police oppression. Eventually, this small inconspicuous café seemed to gain strength from all the negative attention and morphed into a sanctuary for youths and adults alike. It was a kind of refuge for those who felt expelled from what might best be described as the normal workings and institutions of society.

Ultimately, the rigorous stop and search regime in the area, the constant events of police harassment and brutality became the usual unwelcome formula for igniting the literal flames of resentment and rage. It was inevitable that social unrest would prevail; the youths, the community had had enough, it was a night where one too many felt victimised and the infamous St Pauls riots was born.

My brother left the youth club with a friend without my knowledge which at the time sent a bolt of worry through me. Danger and violence were erupting all around. It left me unable to keep an eye on him, to protect him, look after him in case he needed me. Instinct told me I needed urgently to get him back. This event was to lead to more than just being baffled and little did I know that much later it would be a part of my final conversation with my brother.

Things in the family home seemed relatively happy during my youth in the 1970's.

Although my parents sometimes had arguments then made up, this seemed a normal part of family life. Until a bombshell hit. It seemed so sudden, out of the blue. In 1979, after 25 plus years of marriage, my parents divorced.

I was devastated to say the least; from my teenage perspective, after the initial blame games and arguments, I was still unclear why they had to divorce in the first place. I sometimes wondered if they knew.

After a long period of time, they eventually became and remained amicable friends until the end of their lives. I was a perplexed 14-year-old. I remember my feelings of physical and emotional helplessness and the sense of protection for my young brother I had developed was magnified.

By the time of the divorce my eldest brother was living his own life away from the family home with his own family and I was suddenly thrust into the role of being man about the house.

Looking back, I'm not sure if I just took on this new role because it was vacant or because it was expected of me. I had a new responsibility as protector and safety officer for my mom, older sister and more importantly my younger brother. I was going to protect and keep everyone from harm.

David, my youngest brother, was 4 years younger than I, and the youngest of four siblings. I was the second youngest, then there was my older sister, Jillana, who was a year and six months older than me, and our eldest brother was our eldest sibling, Ronald, who was 8 years my senior.

In the early 1970's I was responsible for escorting and dropping off my little brother at the local nursery on my way to my junior school. My brother would loudly bawl every time I had to leave him there. He wanted me to stay but of course I couldn't.

Growing up, my brother's friends were made up mainly of the younger siblings of my friends. We were like a family. My brother and I were best of friends; we never argued or fought. We went on to attend separate secondary schools, my brother to Monks Park and I to Bishopston.

One sunny afternoon, on the way home from school my brother and his school friends were set upon by a school bully and his mates who attended his school. The bullying occurrence took place in a park that was used by my brother as a short home from school.

Providentially, I happened to be walking home through the park at the same time as the bully was expressing his aggressive, unkind nature rather too confidently towards my brother and his mates. I naturally intervened, as older brothers do, let's just say my brother and his mates were never bothered by that nasty bully again.

Throughout our teenage and adolescent years, we shared interests in cycling, roller hockey and roller-skating in general. Together with our friends we both shared in the joys of roller skating through the streets of and parks of Bristol and surrounding counties.

Right up until my brother's late teens and beyond, I always felt a strong sense of duty to always be there for him, ready to protect him from harm, big brother protecting the younger one. It seemed normal.

Over time however, David's main sport became basketball. He still roller skated and dabbled in a bit of boxing now and again. In my eyes as he grew older, he certainly had the stature and skills of a basketball player, all 6 feet 3 inches of him. I would jokingly refer to him and his mates who were all a similar towering height, and younger than me, of the McDonald generation. My pet theory at the time was that those with a super tall height grew because of eating too many Big Macs. Maybe it was just my way of rationalising how these youths were shooting up in height like bean stalks. Who knows?

Like my father, my brother had a love of working with wood. He couldn't resist the smell of freshly cut pine wood. Over his adult years he worked as a chippy on a variety of projects which he enjoyed. A chip off the old block, one could say.

At the time of the deeply traumatic experience that later affected me, it felt like I was going through not one, but a relentless series of harrowing events. The late Queen described it well with her infamous quote: Annus horribilis. The translation from Latin is 'horrible year'.

Nonetheless, although not apparent to me at the time, the events in the year 2001 - my annus horribilis - became a valuable lesson from which I learnt so much.

The experience made me realise how the mind can become the body's worst enemy. Yet, conversely, the mind could also become the body's greatest healer. Over time, I was able to recognise how an acidic mindset could lead me to lose vitality and health. By changing my state of my mind, I have been able to transform my ailing body back to a state of balance. I chose to go on this healing journey without the use of conventional pharmaceutical drugs or medication.

> *A wise man should consider that health is the greatest of human blessings and learn how, by his own thoughts, to derive benefit from his illness.* Hippocrates

My school summer holidays during the late 1970s also involved searching for slow worms in their habitat. I had read a book about them, and my young impressionable mind became fascinated by the thought of catching one.

I would go along the dangerously steep, grassy railway embankment, not far from my home. There used to be a disused waiting room on the platform, which was overgrown with shrubbery and nettles; it was said to be haunted. For me and my friends though, this was a safe place to be, providing a great place to play; trains took forever to arrive and sometimes they never did. If a train did arrive it was a freight train where its top speed was usually between five and ten miles per hour. It would sometimes just come to a standstill and wait with its cargo of cow hide and coal.

When the sun was high, we would go scrumping – or picking fruits - along the embankment, chopping with sticks through stinging nettles and the long grass, imagining being in a jungle. We were searching for the delicious juicy apples, plums and pears that hung over garden walls, adjacent to the grassy railway bank.

Our fruity pickings would replace breakfast, lunch and sometimes dinner; what we couldn't eat, we'd bring home and share with family and friends. It was too good to waste.

As I grew older, I became more adventurous. It is surprising how two wheels and a pair of handlebars can open out an astonishing new world; I would join my friends on lengthy cycle rides to places that seemed light years away from our urban existence. The smell of cow dung and vegetation would fill our nostrils as we cycled to our limits. A feeling that I can only describe as ecstatic exhaustion would take over. By the time I reached my late teens I had become a fully-fledged adventurer who loved the outdoors.

I took pleasure in finding my way down to the Avon Gorge, a place where I would go rock climbing with my climbing partner, Pete. I discovered that clinging to a rock, three hundred feet up on a ledge, was rather awe-inspiring. It gave me an adrenaline rush that I couldn't get from the usual teenage frolics. It was then that I learned to respect the rock face, nature, and my life. They all possess a raw, untouched beauty of their own individual making. There they lie, so often undiscovered, or overlooked without thought whenever they are stumbled upon.

Over time, roller-skating became a new passion. It happened unexpectedly after a visiting relative from the USA gave me a pair of roller skates as a gift. Here was another simple contraption on wheels. I would roller-skate day and night, and it seemed at times as if I wore my skates more often than I wore my shoes.

I used to practice all kinds of manoeuvres, like the barrel roll, different jumps, and spinning through air techniques. Over time, I became skilled enough to become a member of a local roller hockey team, The Strollers. Sounds 1960's, a local pop group in the age of the Beatniks. However, we eventually became good enough to be entered into a local league, where we won and lost matches, and we always had fun. Great stuff.

In due course, I developed an interest in the martial arts, kick, and amateur boxing. Participating in these sports gave me a great sense of self-confidence and self-discipline, enhancing my natural respect for others. At 19 years' old I became an active boxer and a member of the amateur boxing association (ABA) circuit. So far, so good.

Unfortunately, although I was progressing rather well as a capable boxer, I had to retire from the sport due to recurring injuries to a bone in my right hand. Nonetheless, it was during this time of rest and reflection when I seriously considered what I could offer society, in terms of making it a better place.

My mind went back to when I had left school and I had worked as a labourer, renovating old houses, but now I wanted to do something more challenging. I was becoming conscious of helping the underprivileged and disadvantaged in my community, and in 1983 I started working as a community sports leader. It was doing this where I began to gain experience in how leisure activity could be used to empower, build self-esteem, and motivate vulnerable members of society. It was a revelation and produced a good feeling.

These people were not without hope. They had something good to offer.

Whilst employed in this post I worked as a volunteer for a local probation service; it was aimed at young people and where I would be involved with offering programmes of activities as an alternative to custody.

About eighteen months later I took up the offer of a job in London as a residential support worker, working with young adults from a variety of backgrounds with a range of complex needs.

Over time, it became increasingly noticeable that the effects of regular exercise coupled with a good diet produced optimistic results in the wellbeing of the young people whom I worked with. Exercise seemed to 'exorcise' a troubled spirit as well as enhance positive change in the mind and body. Yet there were no drugs or medication involved in this. It was a natural pathway.

In the late 1990s I continued to observe the favourable results that could be gained from participating in some form of exercise, especially to individuals experiencing mental health issues. It was as if the body possessed the answer to its own problem. Physical could transform mental and it would not suppress the underlying issues but rather, transform them into new and better energy.

Throughout my work as an exercise instructor to these clients, I noticed how members of this group were able to transcend from a place of low esteem and depression to a place where they felt good about themselves and generally more positive. Their outlook on life was different. It was like a spotlight had been shone into their lives, illuminating something that had been sitting there already, untapped, and undiscovered.

2

Selective Hearing

By 2001, I was in my 2nd year of studying Sports Science at the University of Surrey, and in the evenings and on my days off, I worked part time for a community care employment agency. My aim was to set up something of my own that could offer help in the form of therapeutic exercise for the underprivileged.

Everything was going ok, and I was coping well with work and the demands of my studies. However, what I was to experience that year, made me begin to look at life through a completely different pair of proverbial glasses.

On the evening of the 2nd, March 2001, I was repairing a punctured bicycle wheel in my flat, in pensive mood.

I loved cycling and wanted to get my mountain bike back on the road. It still gave me so much pleasure and freedom to go where I wanted; besides, my bike kept me active and took me to work.

In the meantime, my head nodded gently in time to the rhythmical tunes that were radiating from the radio perched on a shelf in my kitchen.

As I squeezed the thick rubber plaster against the skin of the black inner tube to cover the tiny perforation, my concentration was suddenly broken by unrelated thoughts that entered my head.

I remembered my next-door neighbour, Albert. He was in his eighties, and he still moved about looking strong and mobile and he wore a tough facial expression. He was a slightly built man, not very tall, and he walked with a confident swagger.

Albert was kind and gracious, always optimistic, and cheerful; he was much younger in spirit than his chronological age. Whenever he got the chance Albert would tell me about his lucky escape during World War II, and how he lost some of his comrades from enemy fire. I could sometimes see the sadness in his glazed cataract eyes. He was one from that generation, stoic, resilient, get on with it, I survived, millions didn't.

Albert was always watching out for me and asking if I was ok, the old soldier in him was still alive, emanating an air of protection and security.

Then, suddenly, the blaring of the phone abruptly dislocated me from my thoughts. For some reason, the ringing tone seemed to have a rhythm of urgency and alarm. You remember the oddest of things looking back because it even seemed to ring in tune to the up-tempo music playing in the background, *brr-brr, brr-brr, brr-brr.*

After lowering the volume of the music, I picked up the receiver and placed it to my ear; the voice on the other end of the line was familiar to me, yet sounded alien, excitability, a rush of words, agitated. Alarmingly, I detected a cloak of fear, anguish, dread, the words thrown at me in a quick, frantic tone; there were no hellos or the usual telephone etiquette, 'How are you, how's things?'

'He's dead, your brother David, he's dead, they shot him!'

Unable to digest this, my instant thought was that it was a misdialled number or that someone was playing a prank.

'Who is this? I asked.

'It's me, your father!' He carried on, his words in one long stream. 'Your brother is dead!' he yelled down the phone. 'They shot him. David, he's dead! DEAD!'

From experience in my youth, I had often noticed that when my father's words were draped in a much stronger Jamaican accent than usual, it usually meant one thing, trouble.

His words penetrated my skull like daggers of iced steel. What?

Nevertheless, I remained calm. I wasn't quite ready to digest such a horrible lump in one sentence. Something else must be going on.

'Hold on a minute,' I replied, keeping my voice steady. I was deliberately exercising a kind of selective hearing. His short outburst was too much information, too quickly. I needed to take this in and slow it down. Something wasn't right and it would all be put right if I heard the right words. Everything was fine.

I couldn't possibly have heard it correctly; it had been said in a rapid, incoherent babble. My brother had fallen and hurt himself, he would be mildly injured and soon be up and running again.

'Can you repeat what you said, please?' I asked him.

My father's voice was almost howling at me. Distraught. 'Yuh bruddah! Him dead! They shot him! David dead.'

The words began writhing and twisting, going right inside every core of my being, penetrating places I didn't know I had. It was like a slow ugly digestion, a rotten meal, something that tasted foul. A sour, repugnant untruth that needed to be believed.

Within a few seconds, I was on the floor. I bent over on my knees, a tiny child. Vulnerable, a force gone, a link too valuable to break, like a snapped chain that could never be healed. Yet strangely complacent.

Then shock took over, doing its job in an overwhelming flow. Water going beyond its normal limits, cascading in an angry torrent onto dry land, banks bursting in an explosion of destruction. I was crying like I had never cried before.

During my boxing career, I had often been engaged in a friendly sparring session with a fellow boxer. That was normal, enjoyable, an involuntary, floor experience. Happy. Not this. Not tumbling down, a dishevelled rag, carelessly ripped in half. Destroyed.

A strange ringing in my ears dulled all sense of what was happening. Then came a caving in of my lower limbs, automatic, like a vehicle out of control, ending up in a crashed heap of twisted metal. A cold sweat began breaking out all over me. My arms shuddered with the cold, an icy ripple travelling to my feet tucked somewhere beneath me. It could have been the middle of a hot summer; I could have been anywhere. I wanted to be anywhere. Anywhere but here, on this floor, trying to take in a piece of news that could be delivered in a few words. My brother had been shot and killed. The taste of adrenalin in my mouth felt bitter, like raw orange peel. It filled my senses. Then I suddenly had it. Of course. I had sustained an unwelcome left hook to my chin, that's what had put me on the canvas. It's why I was where I was at this moment. Pwang! Out. Blast.

Only this time it wasn't a friendly spring left hook to my chin. No punches had been thrown, I had not been hoodwinked by a clever left hook, I had been brought to the floor by an unspeakable intrusion, hurtling at me in the dark, an ominous body blow. The emotionally charged words were spilling out from my father's mouth like gurgling oil.

In between my gut-wrenching cries, oblivious to the disturbance to my neighbours, I felt as though something had exploded inside me, rising from the deep, from that place in the soul that has no name. In the beat of a second, I had been reduced to a broken creature, without power. I had gone, melted into a pot. Hopelessly insurmountable, I had been pulled into a void, mired in dread.

'No…No…No…NO!'

In the second it takes to fire a bullet from a gun, hitting its target full on, in the blink of 1 second, my world had exploded. It had changed from the relative peace and calm of day-to-day living to a turmoil of despair. A foreign land stretched ahead, leading at that moment to a charred and blackened future. I was unprepared for anything like this.

When my senses at last decided to return to a scrap of normal, I asked myself, 'How? How can this be true?' I shut down, refusing to believe anything more that night. I knew instinctively what I needed to do. I had to see the body of my brother with my own eyes. I needed to know in all its stark, growling reality, that it was true.

I was now beginning to experience something else, an intense and exaggerated feeling of protectiveness for the rest of my family. The lion who had lost a key member of the pack. At the same time, I felt that I had to do what was right.

Reluctantly, I knew I must squeeze myself into the proverbial pigeonhole that society had prepared for me. Yes, I told myself, grinding my teeth, I had to take revenge. I am not a violent man. I am not a cruel, bitter, aggressive man. I am not deliberately vindictive. For a moment, I contemplated. I paused momentarily, refusing to accept the torturing thought that I would have to go against my nature. Revenge was a difficult word, loaded with too much…and it was loaded with my brother.

What needed to be done before anything else was for me see my brother's body. No one had yet seen him, I reasoned with myself, it doesn't have to be him. I cleared my mind and attempted to be optimistic, to rationalise what was happening. Sliding into denial is common. Perhaps there was mistaken identity, someone who had a similar name, same age, living in the same district. A disfigured ugly thing to happen to anyone. Someone's husband, father, son. Anyone, please, but not my brother. As far as I was concerned, until I had personally seen my brother, he would still be alive.

I arrived in Bristol the following evening and found myself volunteering to be the person who would formally identify the body. The family police liaison officer who led me to the mortuary entrance had a calm, supportive presence about him, for which I was grateful.

I was functioning on a strange, robotic level, merely going through the motions because everything around me was surreal, like being in a movie. It's what you see on the television, in the cinema; it doesn't happen in real life and not to a close and loving member of your family.

One moment I was at home in London mending my push bike...and here I was outside a Bristol morgue waiting with other family members and friends to identify my brother who, purportedly, was dead. Couldn't he be just a tiny bit alive? Enough to whisk him into A & E, resuscitate, bring him back to life, stuttering, gasping for breath, heart beating.

I was a character in the movie, being watched, observed, guided, and all I could do was to go with the flow and follow the script. Couldn't we have another take? The script altered, a better, brighter script. But not this.

I walked into the morgue. I looked at the figure laid out in front of me, wishing only that I could turn away and didn't have to look. A life obliterated.

Yes, it was him. I softly closed my eyes before leaning over and kissing the forehead of my brother's motionless body. The script was before me, seeing my brother lying so still, so quiet. The pulse of electric, beat by beat, that had once been emitted from this giant frame that lay before me was no more. He had left me.

I turned and slowly approached the exit door to the chapel of rest; the door was opened by the liaison officers, and I looked into the eyes of everyone standing on the other side of it.

The faces of my mother, father, elder brother, sister, and friend, seemed to be filled with an expectant hope. Everything would be alright, I could see it in their faces; they were straining to hear me say those words that would bring smiles, relief, it was all fine. But their expressions could not hide their fear and their sorrow. It wasn't going to be alright.

They must have read my motionless face. It wasn't difficult. You don't emerge from that with a smile of greeting, not even a nervous laugh. You emerge empty. Defeated. Stripped of power. Irreversible. There is nothing you can do.

The room seemed to visibly darken. And still they all seemed to be silently begging me to release them from their anguish, to tell them that it wasn't his body that lay there. It was someone else, just as we all had thought, mistaken identity. Some other poor family would bear the load. Not us.

Afraid to speak, I stood rigid. I feared the wrong words or sounds would escape from my mouth, a nervous stupid response. Sorry, folks, that's it. Banal and meaningless. I simply nodded to each person present. No words were needed. No shouting, no scream, no dissolving into tears. I was merely acknowledging what was needed to be acknowledged, that it was my brother's lifeless body that was lying there in that room. No more than this simple nod of the head. I will never, to the end of my days, forget that scene.

Shock eventually recedes, dissipating into a cloud of non-living, a foggy grey damp. What followed was the process of grieving, long and individual, different for each of us. At times spontaneous, at times subdued, deeply personal, letting no man in.

The reality stunned me. It was as if someone had shot a poison dart through me, anaesthetising, freezing my senses yet failing to delete the pain. Emotion liquefied, then became gaseous, spirited into a barren land. Disbelief colliding with belief. My sense of hearing became muffled to the sounds around me. For all that, a tiny spark, a life force borne of man's supreme will to keep going at all costs, took possession. I managed to hold it together. I survived. With my brother still next to me, living with me, I pulled through.

3

Rumours

The funeral was a tremendous affair. He would have loved to have seen it, how he would have smiled. It was attended by several hundred people, including family and friends from the UK, some of whom had travelled from faraway places like Jamaica, USA, Canada, Greece, Spain, and Holland.

People from all over the world and from all backgrounds were there, classmates from years ago, schoolteachers from my brother's past, colleagues, friends and, I suspect a few enemies too. The plain clothes family liaison officers were there too. What a life, what a man, loved by all.

During the service, I was standing at the pulpit, and beside me stood a close friend, called Dave. He would be my voice that day, I had decided. He was going to read a poem which I had dedicated to my brother. Had I attempted to do this myself, I knew I would have broken up, the emotion swallowing me whole. I am enormously grateful for my friend's kind gesture. I simply could not have read it out aloud myself.

As we stood together in the large, overcrowded church, stuffed full of so many people, all there to pay their respects, to reflect and to remember, my mind was beginning to race. How were my mother and father feeling? They were always dignified and composed, and it was hard to tell.

While the ceremony took place, I could not help being distracted in my thoughts. Questions kept occupying my mind. They were important questions, ones I needed to answer for my brother's sake, as well as my own. Where was the man or men who had ended his life? Who had pulled the trigger? Why had they felt the need to do this? My worst thought of all was wondering if they were present, here in the church, quietly observing? It was not a comfortable thought.

As these questions filtered into my mind, the service continued; I could feel my love, my inner balance being shrouded by resentment, pain, anger, and retribution. I felt that I should be doing something, planning, and preparing for the inevitable, an eye for an eye, a tooth for a tooth. Love for my brother overpowered me whilst these thoughts crept through my mind. How could anyone get away with this? How could they be allowed to continue enjoying their life?

People came to give their respects, offering condolences; unfortunately, there were also a few who gave their imagined and exaggerated account of what had happened to my brother and why. Some so-called friends were even fighting with each other to get their hearsay theories heard by those who chose to listen. Rumours were circling that my brother's killing was drugs related; others said it was simply because of jealousy and bad mindedness, while others merely said he was in the wrong place at the wrong time. I did not know what to make of any of these theories. Speculation, rumour, when I needed truth.

'If you feel so strongly about expressing your version of events and really want to help, then why don't you go and do the right thing like telling the authorities?' someone would exclaim. Then there would be silence.

I had no clue as to why my brother was killed, and I wasn't interested in listening to gossip and hearsay. All I wanted was the truth. For him, for myself, for the huge well of love I had for him, and still do, for the gap that could never be filled.

In the meantime, I was happy to just take a back seat and stay low in the shadows, calmly observing, contemplating. I would subtly observe and gather the information that I felt relevant, before trying to make sense out of the nonsense. For nonsense, it surely was.

As the shovels patted the mound of red dirt into place, those who were still there, stood around the grave and continued to sing renditions of Bob Marley songs. However, David's music taste was not merely limited to Bob Marley.

He had a wide range of taste in music. The genres which he listened to included Soul and Jazz Funk. His favourite was always Hip Hop with artists such as Puff Daddy, Snoop, Biggie & Tupac, and others. I recalled how he enjoyed listening to the style of reggae tunes that he would hear me play.

Standing opposite me on the other side of the graveside next to my mom an elderly lady suddenly burst into song. Her voice sounded so mature and youthful, and her powerful voice silenced the murmuring of the crowd.

Bob Marley's 'No Woman No Cry echoed across the graveyard, and by the second verse, her singing would take on a call-and-response element with the gathered crowd responding to her every note and verse, as if rehearsed. It was mesmerising.

'Every Thing's Gonna Be Alright' and 'One Love' followed. Then other popular reggae, folk/spiritual songs by various reggae artists rang through the air. Garnet Silk's 'Christ in His Kingly Character', and Luciano's 'Your World and Mine' energised the bright morning air. It was a celebration of David's life. It could not have been done better if it had been strictly rehearsed beforehand. It was spontaneous, respectful, and so full of love.

To add to the significance, on that day the sun was shining in a perfect cerulean blue sky. Goodbye David, goodbye my friend. While in my heart I knew it would never be goodbye. He would always be with me, saying Hello.

After the funeral, it is when the grieving process really begins. My mind was going into a kind of rapid rewind, reliving, playing through familiar scenes of our life together, over again like a video. It was as if I was trying to salvage and secure the final memories I had of David.

He was a giant of a man. One of those men who radiate a bullish strength, whilst retaining the gentle spirit of a real man. He was six feet two inches tall and built like a prize fighter who one might glimpse in old movies, the kind of man you might think would go on forever. Yet, despite his frame, he was respectful, compassionate, a real gentleman. He had it all. He had his life before him. How could this have happened? *How?*

4

Dreams

Only the weekend before he died, I had been sitting with him in his apartment. We had joked and talked, the way only 2 brothers can do. We were both so full of life, in all its glamour and hardship. We reminisced, days gone by, things we had done together and enjoyed…days before the time when he would be so brutally, so violently and without warning snatched away. How poignant it all seemed now. If only I had known…

We didn't see each other as often as we would have liked; it's always like that when you grow into adults. Lives begin to separate, forking onto new pathways, independence arrives yet you know you are always there, each in his own place. That day, we had time for one another. We had enjoyed each other's company, laughing and chatting, enjoying time for what it was, young enough not to care. Now, I wish we had cared, I wish we had seen the precious reality, counting every second. That brief pocket of time felt more sacred, more meaningful and special than any other, because it was the last time we would spend together. If I had known, could have glimpsed the future, would I have acted differently, said more, not said more?

How could I have known? He only, then, had days left to live.

Uncannily, it seems as though the universe had known all along that our infrequent and joyful moment together would be our last. Perhaps it did. It had only been barely a week later that he had called me in the morning for the final time. I remember thinking that it was unusually early in the day for my brother to call me.

'You're lucky to have caught me, yuh know,' I said. 'It's my day off today, I would usually be in work by now.'

'You were meant to be there, that's why,' he said, 'to hear what I want to ask you.'

'Yes, I guess you're right about that,' I said and added, brightly, 'Ok, what's up?'

'You have to help me, bro,' he said. I noticed a concerned tone to his voice. Holding my breath in anticipation, I eventually blurted out, 'Yes, ok, go on, ask me then, what is it?'

'I had a dream and I want you to interpret it for me,' he replied. 'It was so real, and I believed that it meant something special.'

I explained to my brother that I was not 'Mystic Meg' a celebratory clairvoyant who used to be on national television.

I couldn't predict dreams, but he insisted that this time I could. 'I know that you can interpret this for me,' he pleaded, 'and I'm begging you to, please.'

At last, I gave in. 'Alright brother, go on then, tell me what your dream was about?'

After listening to the vivid description of my brother's dream...which involved a bright golden shower of light, I was surprised at how easily my imagination put together a meaning surrounding the narrative of his dream.

'Your dream is very clear to me,' I ventured. 'I can only really describe what it would mean if I had such a dream.'

'Ok, so what would it mean for you?'

'In a nutshell,' I said while sensing his anticipation as he listened in silence. 'This sounds like there's going to be a great change...the end of something old and familiar, but the start of something new.'

'Yes!' he exclaimed excitedly. 'That's it, yeah! That's exactly it.' He sounded so animated, so pleased I had confirmed his own feelings. 'I knew you could do it, respect! Brother, thank you!' His jubilant tone sounded as if he had just won a million.

My brother's reaction to my interpretation led me to the assumption that he had received confirmation of something big about which he had already known deep down. I was happy for him, and felt relief that I could fulfil his request, however extraordinary it was. As we talked, somewhere in our conversation we would always acknowledge the mutual benefits that we had gained from our last weekend together.

It was made even more touching because it had been filled with a special intensity in our spoken words, of the shared love that we had not expressed before; it had all been spoken, not with the flippancy of youth, carefree words that had been loosely tossed in the air, 'yeah, man luv yer too.' No, the exchange had been spoken with a ripe maturity, a caring honesty borne of deep sentiment and warmth. An unbreakable bond, welded like steel, and which no man could break apart.

With sensitivity, we discussed when the day would come when we would need to carry our parents to their final resting place. Little did I know then that the script would very soon have an alternative plot, one that neither of us could have imagined. For instead, it would be I who ended up carrying my brother to his final physical resting place.

On that weekend it was as if we had been allocated time to bond as adults, just as we had done in our youth, an acknowledgement that adulthood would not change anything, no matter how our lives might diverge, whether we married and had children of our own or relocated with our jobs. That day, we confirmed the bond between us as grown men, and we both knew deep down where it counts that it really could not ever be broken. Even if life took us to different ends of the earth.

Although he was younger than me, we had shared so many experiences together. I began to recall, almost magically, days of summers gone by when we used to entertain ourselves at the neighbourhood adventure playground. This place was at times dangerous, where 'pinecone battles' were common amongst friends. Unfortunately, though, on a rare occasion, someone would throw the odd stone instead of a pinecone.

Bonfires were a regular spectacle, due to locals who lived in the neighbourhood dumping scrap wood and old furniture there, as they knew it would be burnt. In the nearby field, unusual games of football would take place. Well, they were more like a mixture of wrestling, boxing and rugby, a bit like the popular mob football of seventh century England.

However, although these games looked rather wild and untamed to the observer, injuries were surprisingly low, and it was quite disciplined when you considered the rough and tumble of the game.

Sometimes my brother and I would play cricket matches in the street with friends. I can remember one of our uncles joining in one of the games; he was a tall, slim man, called Reggie.

Reggie's lively and unconventional ways, with his red, yellow, and green woolly hat, made him a popular figure in the local community, and he had many acquaintances, both young and old.

It was my turn to bat and my uncle decided to bowl.

'Let me teach you youths a little thing or two about cricket,' he exclaimed, brightly confident.

As he ran towards me, he let the tennis ball fly from his hand like a rocket. I raised my bat in anticipation and imagined that I was Viv Richard, a phenomenal West Indian cricket player of the 1970's.

As the tennis ball left my uncle's fast rotating palm, it flew towards the makeshift wicket which was made of a short thin plank of plywood. I struck the ball with my cricket bat, and…*Blap!*

The tennis ball sailed high through the air like a rocket but unfortunately ended up piercing through an upstairs window of the house opposite, across the road. The window was closed at the time, which meant it hit the glass full on. The sound of shattering, breaking glass was muffled by the curtains behind it; small pieces tinkling down like diamonds in the afternoon sun.

All the children who were present, as well as me, simultaneously disappeared in flight as fast as our youthful legs could carry us.

Later that day I learned that my uncle had offered to repair the broken window, and everything was okay again.

All these thoughts were channelling through my mind after David's funeral. The fun, the silly things like how we crafted homemade Go Carts created from old prams wheels, wooden boxes, and six-inch nails. They were once the must have plaything of the day and we cherished them. In those days I don't recall there being any notion of health and safety policies to keep us safe from harm, and we seemed to be continually at the mercy of the gods.

Although we were surrounded by so much potential danger as we played, the casualties were small.

I was still always on the lookout for my brother's wellbeing, because he was my younger brother, but also because I was responsible for him, and if he was hurt in any way then I would have had to answer to my mother.

On that last day I was to see him alive, chatting, reminiscing, enjoying the nostalgia of times gone by, by brother and I continued to delve into the days of our youthful playground adventures. We were lost in a boyhood world of carefree. We recalled a boy going by the nickname, Gut. It had been one those sunny Saturday afternoons when he came running into the adventure playground making a happy wooing sound, mimicking a train or airplane. It's what kids do.

Unfortunately, Gut was unaware that an older boy, whose name was Brownie, had just hurled a large thin sheet of scrap Formica into the air for fun. Like a boomerang it soared upward through the warm air. Gut skipped through the adventure playground gates like a young gazelle, unaware of the gliding danger above. The menacing piece of Formica was now descending speedily like a bird of prey swooping down for its kill.

Like a guided missile, the Formica finally connected with Gut's head, and although it was a bloody and tearful end to the drama, Gut was blessed with only receiving seven stitches to his forehead. It was one of those situations where we could laugh at now, but it could have ended so differently.

My brother and I had continued to talk about these things, some of which were so deep and personal. We discussed truths that had always been at the back of our minds but never mentioned. It was a glorious day. It was not the sort of day to be repeated every week, or even every month. It was that which made it even more special. A golden piece of time to treasure. More worthy now than a piece of gold. I hold it in my memory where it will stay forever. Our last time together, the last time I would hear his voice, see his big healthy frame, eat with him, laugh with him. The last time I would see him alive.

I brought myself back to the present, the funeral over at last. David had died. He was now buried. Yet I had not wanted to lose him completely. The whole business of the funeral process had made me realise that memories were all that was left. It was as if holding these tiny loose threads so close to me could somehow deny the reality of the event which I had just pulled myself through. As I further reminisced about David and I and the past, I became aware of how my mind was drifting in and out from the present to the past. I was holding on to a fragment, something that could unite the two, make it less real, soften what could never be softened but I did not want it to go stale and hard either, a dusty old piece of crust, pushed aside, forgotten, get on with your life now. I knew that could never be. I loved David too much. The shock was still raw.

On that day when we chatted, I recall deciding to let my brother know that I had borrowed a tent from a guy called Rick, who was a mutual friend. I had suggested to him that we could both go on a survival weekend together.

'Just you and me, and nature, how about it?' I suggested to him.

David nodded, almost imperceptibly, taking in what I had just said.

'We could drive out into the countryside and find a bit of wilderness, you know, get closer to the natural elements, the wind, the rain, and the stars,' I went on, enthusing to my idea as I went.

As I spoke, I could sense David's subtle reaction to my unexpected proposition.

A loud silence fell on both of us. We gazed at each other for a few seconds. Then, out of nowhere, we began to laugh like loud, boisterous schoolboys.

What I had expressed was so unexpected and out of the blue that it had resulted in laughter. How I now wanted to capture that sound of laughter. David's chuckles ringing through my mind now, after the funeral. It was as if he were here now, beside me, still laughing.

'We should do this, you know,' I went on, as I composed myself, wondering why we were so amused.

'Yes,' David replied. 'I know, and that would be a good thing to do when the weather gets a bit warmer.'

Eventually, we submitted to our laughter and continued sipping Hennessey. Once the laughter had faded, we had begun to contemplate the likely night clubs that we could attend later in the evening that weekend.

We then relaxed into the evening, our bellies bulging from our afternoon feast of West Indian chicken soup, with dumplings, yams, and green banana.

When we eventually resumed our conversation, out of the blue, my brother said, 'I want to say sorry, you know?' he said.

'Sorry,' I said, a little surprised. 'What for?'

David had then taken me back to the year 1981 when there had been a riot in the city. The evening sky had been a glow of red, orange, and grey. The smell of toxic smoke tinted the evening air, and the sounds of sirens could be heard blaring in the distance. It did not look good.

Our youth club was situated on the very fringes of the disturbances; the failing relationship between the police and local youth was already strained and under intense pressure. It was a feeling of Them v Us.

A friend had alerted me that my brother, with his mate, had left the safety of the club without my knowing. I urgently vacated the club with the speed of a world class sprinter, running to catch them up, before they reached the danger zone. Worry for my brother, and of course his friend, were pounding through my head. My sense of protection was like a rocket-powered missile.

By chance, and about two hundred yards ahead of me, against the backdrop of the illuminated air, I could see the silhouette of two, vulnerable looking human frames. It was them. There was no time to feel relief. I had to catch up and pull them back.

I quickly caught up with my brother and his mate, seemingly determined on their dangerous liaison ahead.

'What the hell did you think you were doing, leaving the club like that without my knowing?' I stupidly scolded on the spot. 'Don't you realise how dangerous it is up ahead?'

My brother nodded and with some more admonishment, agreed to come back with his friend to the club.

Hastily, we walked back up the steep hill towards the sanctuary of the youth club. In that moment, I became aware of a sound; I recognised it as the sound of a revving engine, and it was coming from behind and close.

Words of racial hatred emanated from the same direction of the sound of the revving engine. The sinister, growling motor was now much closer than before. Urgency was thick in the air. In the next minute, I felt a sudden blow to the back of my head.

The vehicle sped away as quickly as it came. My large, afro styled hair became saturated like a sponge in blood.

'Run, now!' I shouted to both my brother and his friend 'Quick!' In rapid time my brother, his friend and I managed to reach the safety of the youth club again.

As we talked that last day together, David wasn't rambling, and I could see he was genuinely trying to express an emotion that could probably never be put into words. I had only done what instinct had told me. I had protected him, received a blow to my head…it had healed, I had not been dreadfully injured and nothing more needed to be said, I was alive and well. I had not suffered concussion or brain damage.

'Look,' I said, trying to reason with him. 'That incident took place several decades ago, you were young and curious, who can blame you for walking off.'

He did not speak.

'I never imagined for one moment you were at fault,' I said as he listened to me, head bowed. 'And I'm sorry that you have been blaming yourself for it all these years.'

He raised his chin and looked at me with a deprecating smile.

'Believe me, David,' I went on, regardless of his silence, 'when I say right now, today, that you were not to blame for what happened, ok?' I was good heartedly admonishing him, whilst doing my best to reassure him. I wanted him to banish this thought, once and for all. 'It wasn't your fault,' I said, smiling at him. 'You are my younger brother and I'll always feel responsible for your wellbeing, whatever the circumstances.'

To lighten the atmosphere, I said, a little cheekily, 'Furthermore, I was glad that it happened to me and not to you or your friend.'

He looked at me.

'Well,' I said. 'Your heads were much smaller than mine, and I don't think they would have absorbed the blow as well as mine did.'

His face broke into a broad smile.

Then we broke into loud laughter. My brother's face was alight with his familiar big beaming smile.

'We survived a troubled time,' I said with resignation. 'And I was being serious when I said that you weren't to blame for anything that had happened.'

Yet still he insisted, 'Nevertheless, I will make it up to you one day, because you saved my life.'

5

Assassin

At the time, I had been expecting David to apologise for the pranks he used to play on me – although in truth we were both guilty of that. There had been the time when David knew jolly well that I had just completed a 12-hour gruelling night shift doing a stint of security work and that my bedtime was 7am. Unfortunately, David didn't quite see it this way. He saw it as a time to put my self-control to the test before he set off to work. For me, it became a trial of strength.

He would deliberately, and slowly, start crunching up empty crisp packets as I tried to settle to sleep. This scrunchy crackle is surprisingly loud when you're exhausted after a night on duty in desperate need of some humble sleep. That wasn't all. No, that wasn't enough for his scope of practical jokes, he wanted to make more mischief. He would then begin clapping his lips like a small rodent eating – if you have ever been up close to a small rodent eating. This would be followed by the noisy slurping of tea, a saliva filled, reptilian sucking sound impossible to ignore, then a big *Ahhhhh*. It was all done in a spirit of playful meanness and with the underlying intention of breaking me, to get me to crack. And this was supposed to be brotherly love. Even the closest of brothers can be naughty, I reasoned. And in these moments, David loved to be naughty.

I knew it wasn't going to do me much good to shout at him to stop and that that would likely fuel his fondness for annoying me. If I blew, he would know he had won. Instead, I would grumble quietly and pull the covers over my head, never letting on that his antics were getting the better of me. Take it like a man.

On that final weekend together, I had also been taken by surprise at his need to apologise for something that had happened years ago when we were so young. It was off my radar of thinking. And I had never, since then, given his antics any more thought, dismissing it as brotherly teasing. It wasn't his fault, we were kids. Yet it was almost as if he knew he did not have long left and needed to offload his apology before we would say our final goodbye. His sense of relief at apologising for the youth club incident was palpable.

It was at that point, he reached for the bottle of Hennessy, offered me another drink before slowly pouring one for himself. Topic put to bed with a nightcap.

Without speaking, we touched glasses together and sipped the smooth warm fiery liquid, while nodding our heads in silent agreement that no more needed to be said about the matter.

We continued to immerse ourselves in the act of reminiscing about the good old days, late into that final Saturday evening. Together, we discussed issues relating to God, religious beliefs, politics, war, peace, love, relationships, isms, and schisms.

We reasoned that it was because of human greed, material worship and untamed egos why some of the world's population was suffering. We agreed that 'pigeonhole boxes', and other forms of classifications and stereotyping were illusions of separateness, created for us to feel different, better or worse than our fellow human beings.

We agreed about so much, brothers-in-arms. Just brothers.

After his abrupt exit from the world, so soon after that memorable day, it came streaming back, costing nothing, simple chat, friendship.

On two occasions, strangers whom I had seen for the first time at his funeral invited me to join them for dinner and drinks. They claimed that they were friends of my brother, but my intuitions told me otherwise. I decline these invites because under the circumstances of my demise I needed to be sure who was who. These characters were not only unfamiliar to me, but I later learned that they were also unacquainted with my brother.

Maybe I was being a little paranoid but considering my brother's death and the way he died, I needed to be cautious, my trust in complete strangers was not on my agenda, but I had to be sure who was who and what was their motive.

My concerns were that anyone could come forward and say they were David's friend. But who were the genuine friends of his, who could I trust to give me true and accurate information surrounding his death?

Whatever chit chat was circulating at the time, and there is always a large chunk of this in such situations, no one had been there to witness the terrible deed that had taken place, and no one really knew why it had happened. Speculation and loose chat abound, everyone has an opinion, everyone insists they are right.

All I knew was that my mind was in a place that was unfamiliar to me, I felt obligated to find the killer…or so I thought.

I was chained to this concept, it had become my duty, both to David and to myself. I kept this to myself. No-one but me was aware of these deeper thoughts during this period of lament, and I strained to keep my facial expressions looking friendly and calm. No-one must know what I was thinking inside, what was going on in my head, processing every minute detail. Fortunately, I found I could wear this mask well, an easy task because it was natural for me to be smiling. No-one would guess a thing.

But inside, my thoughts were a mixture of rage and hatred, and it was directed at the character who had ended my brother's life so violently and abruptly. Whoever it was, they needed to be brought to justice.

A great sadness shrouded me whenever I imagined how the rest of my life would be now, without David, and how my family would cope, especially my mother. My mind was constantly being torn between feelings of love and loss in a heady mix with anger and revenge. New and unfamiliar emotions were also beginning to emerge; it was this constant feeling of retribution, and it was growing stronger. I was powerless to stop this, it was like a mechanical whirring, the button pressed with no Stop option. With David's death, the story script of my life had been rewritten; my role, costume and the props had changed, so too had the cast.

In the days and weeks that followed, I received constant offers of information from a variety of people, all claiming to be friends. I remember while drinking in a bar one night, and being approached by a tall, athletically built, attractive female.

Before she left the bar, this woman approached me and whispered in my ear, before kissing me on my cheek, 'If there is anything you need, even a dog, then you should let me know, you can find me here Fridays or Saturdays, in the meantime here's my number.'

In disbelief, I wondered if I had heard and understood this unknown woman correctly. When she mentioned the word 'dog', I was confused. Did it mean a 'dog' as in the animal, a fierce looking hound to protect me, or did she mean 'dog' which was apparently slang for gun.

I found myself beginning to characterise the assassin., I placed him in a play in my head. I could not get it out of my mind that he was still at large, and I believed that he knew of me being in town. I felt that wherever and whoever he was, he now realised that my brother had a family, people who loved him, and a brother.

In the meantime, so infused with anger and retaliation, I was fuelling myself with a diet of alcohol, excess smoking, minimal sleep, and little food which wasn't exactly the healthy kind. To add to this dietary imbalance, I was also exercising intensely; it was like a way of expunging the episode while at the same time reinvigorating my thoughts, so shaded with grey, dark vengeance.

Burning the candle at both ends had never taken on such meaning. And these metaphorical candle ends were in extreme opposition to each other. The situation was dangerous. I was mentally and emotionally veering off-track and down a slippery slope. Oblivion beckoned me. I ignored it.

I was unaware of this at the time, oblivious to being on the edge of the abyss, my mind, body, and spirit out of balance. I was also oblivious to how hazardous to the body being in this state could be.

This relentless daily infliction, like scratching a suppurating wound, is not unsimilar to an addiction, being hooked on gambling or drink, unaware and uncaring of the effect. You are not remotely aware of being in a pit. But slowly, insidiously, my daily activities were poisoning me. It was a conflict going on within, one above the other, vying for supremacy. This daily, groggy activity dulled the pain and filled the void, yet I knew that my mind and body were being deceived. By now, it was impossible to rectify. I had become hollowed out inside.

Somewhere, in the foggy recesses, amidst the grimy, salty mist of my mind, I was striving to make sense of what had happened, the whys and the how's, the what ifs and maybes. My brain was in relentless turmoil, memories of my brother haunted me daily, often out of the blue and without warning. During this time of intense extremes of unhealthy diet and exercise, nothing else in the world seemed to matter. My world had ceased to exist in all but name. I was a shell, a shabby illusion of my former self.

He had been so young, he had not been suffering from a terrible illness, nor had he had an accident; his life had ended, swift, sudden and in a mean, inhuman and dramatic way that was too evil to comprehend.

It seemed ridiculous to dwell on how, in previous years, I had learned how negative thoughts can produce harmful results in the form of acids in your body, but that wasn't at the forefront of my mind right then…and I continued to underestimate the effects of my sinister thoughts.

6

Internal Power

Time moved on and one morning, lying in bed, my eyes opened abruptly, and I felt very much awake. There was a desperate urge to relieve the contents of my full bladder.

It was the early hours of the morning of August 9th, 2001. As my eyes opened, I noticed my bedroom was still dark, apart from the faint orange glow from the streetlights below. There would be several hours yet until the light of dawn. I felt warm beneath my padded quilt, and I flung it off my body, simultaneously springing up out of the bed in my haste to reach the bathroom.

Except that it wasn't quite the leap that I had anticipated. At the same time as I stood upright, I took one natural step forward…and BLAMM! With a heavy thud, I found myself in a crumpled heap on the floor. I'd forgotten all about my bursting bladder by now. Yet, odd though it may seem, I didn't think too much of what had just happened to me, at least not until my clumsy attempt to rise to my feet again.

This is where things became a little tricky. Whenever I tried to stand up, I found myself either flat on my face or rolled over in an awkward jumble on my back.

My thoughts swirled in a kind of calm, dream-like confusion. There was no panic. Instead, I was attempting to rationalise what was happening to me. Quite difficult to rationalise about anything when you're in a kind of flopped-out roll.

Being a sensible sort of person doesn't come easy to me at the best of times and this was going to take all the good sense I possessed. I began with questioning and confirming my whereabouts. Was I having some sort of odd dream, one which was real because I seemed to be in the star, real-life role? I know the mind can play tricks but seriously this was one heck of a trick.

I tried to reason with myself, not that straightforward when you are floating in another world, clinging on to whatever rational thinking you can grasp. 'Try closing your eyes,' I told myself hopefully, whilst awarding myself full marks for functioning on a reasonably logical level at least. 'Because then,' I reasoned, 'you'll wake up all safe again wrapped up in the comfort of your warm bed.' Ah, the bliss.

The problem was, as I lay on the tightly weaved carpeted floor of my room, I was running out of steam. There were only so many comforting questions even I could dream up and ask of myself. Golly, my mind was fast running out of control. As reality, horrible word, began to kick in, things were becoming frightfully apparent. I was wide awake; I wasn't dreaming at all. Crikey.

Things were now looking decidedly different. People called fear and panic loomed up, looking excited. Fear and panic absolutely love these situations, storming in to shove you aside. They thoroughly enjoy taking control. Rather glad that someone is, you let them.

A once peaceful mind was now slowly disintegrating. No, it wasn't, it was fast crumbling. Still, I managed to remain a tiny bit calm, just. Miraculous really. Under the circumstances, I could give myself another little pat on the back. Except that I didn't. The body has powers it doesn't know it has at times. Keep being sensible, I told myself. Keep going. This was getting ludicrous; I wasn't exactly going anywhere. Never mind, I ploughed on, asking myself a few more demanding questions. Was that a stroke I had just experienced? It certainly didn't feel like a stroke of luck. Or maybe I was about to die? Or had I just died? Ah, so there is a heaven, after all. I was in it. For all my terrible misdemeanours, I hadn't gone to the other place, the one with eternal fire. I was ok, God exists, and I would be looked after. More to the point, was I completely losing my mind? I'd lost it.

The questions were rushing around in my head, a whipped-up ice-cream whirlpool of confusion and fear. There's always fear. I became very aware that my physical body felt different. Like a toddler. I was now beginning to feel a real sense of caution sweep through me. Good Heavens, this wasn't like me at all, I'm never cautious; I was the kid who'd gone racing off on his bike to discover new worlds, I'd rolled along on my rollers. Seriously, the Strollers had nothing on this.

When people are about to give up and let panic grab hold of the steering wheel, they sometimes become silly. I became silly. I was an Anansi spider, a mod, rocker, hummingbird, a grotesque creepy crawly; I'd zoomed backwards to a before-life, anything but this. Anything but a hopelessly collapsed blob, scrabbling around on the floor, clinging to the last shreds of hope. And in my desperation, a wild determination was still there, somewhere. I was still resisting the call inside my fluffy mind to surrender. Hand's up, go quietly, don't make a fuss, and keep it clean. Give up now, mate, you've had it.

I made another supreme effort to stand on my feet, using all the strength I possessed which didn't seem like an awful lot. Straining to straighten my knees, the realisation dawned on me that this was going to be an insurmountable feat. Things were not looking good. I couldn't stand. Once more, the body which had always served me so well, did something else. Good thing I had carpet in my room. The piece of jelly that used to be my body collided with the floor like a heavy sack of meat and bones. Me.

Looking like a cross between an amoeba and a fistful of play dough, I managed to roll over onto my back; I was like a little animal learning to take its first steps.

And when people are confronted with terrible fear, they sometimes do odd things, like seeing funny. I'm not sure if what happened next was some sort of nervous reaction, or I had metamorphosed into a giggling looney; it wasn't hard to believe the latter because at that moment I saw funny. Out of the blue, or the pink or whatever, I started laughing. Laughter began gurgling from me, like someone was tickling my feet. As I was already bent double, I was in the ideal spot. Silly little titters mixed with roaring chuckles. Hah, this felt good.

By now, I was looking down at myself from above. Yes, really. I mean, who wouldn't? What I saw wasn't a pretty sight. All six foot, 100kg of me bumbling about on the floor, turning over on an axis looking, frankly, ridiculous. I was a little bemused by this observation. I was even more bemused by my reaction to it, chortling away like a lunatic.

I lost track of time, but I reckoned about 20 minutes to half an hour had passed before I realised that I needed to call out to my flat mate. Reluctantly. She was still asleep in the other room. She was about to get a rude awakening. Something had gone horribly wrong.

'Mary, help!'

No answer.

'MARY!'

This was getting serious. I wondered if I had had a heart attack; any minute now I was about to die. Expunged. Hoovered up. Gone. Good while it lasted. I quickly told myself to be quiet. Shut up, this isn't going to help.

'Mary!' I hollered, trying to subdue those little big signs of panic skipping around in my voice. And by now panic was in its element, thoroughly enjoying the scene. And the panic was about to get worse. It was bursting at the bit to wade in and burst forth, like a bullying line manager.

'Mary, where are you, please come and HELP me!'

Mary entered the living room where I had managed to crawl like a big lumbering insect; I was expending an awful lot of effort in doing this. I can remember seeing the innocence in her eyes and the way her small frame froze. For a moment, she tried to assess the situation and make sense of what was happening. So was I.

The problem was, I could see that Mary was also totally oblivious to my sudden, utter fragility, utterly perplexed at why her fit, young flatmate was crawling about on the floor looking like an idiotic fool. Unsurprisingly, she was a little perplexed. The sight of me lying there on the floor, unable to move as I used to, must have been a bit bewildering.

I looked at her.

She looked at me.

'I can't stand up,' I said feebly.

Silence.

She continued to look at me, struck dumb.

'I don't know what's wrong,' I said, even more feebly. 'My legs are still asleep. My arms are weak, my head feels slightly giddy.' Slightly was putting things mildly.

On my instruction, Mary telephoned the medical help line, NHS direct, a last cling to hopefulness. 111 didn't sound nearly so bad as 999. It took off that terrible word, Emergency. A simple bit of advice would do the trick.

'You need to call an ambulance immediately,' the voice came back down the NHS line.

I shivered. This was it. No, it wasn't, I became stubborn. This was something trivial, a minor matter that in a few minutes would clear. Deep breathe, man. Just relax.

Relax? Hell, this was major. It was looking desperate.

Mary watched as I continued to roll about the place, getting nowhere, except a bit further along the carpet. I kept trying to stand up. I was exhausted. Admit it, mate, this isn't going to work.

Funnily enough, I was still having a good giggle, roaring in miniscule tickly fun. This gave an altogether new meaning to rock 'n' roll. The Rolling Stones had nothing on me. The Rolling Body. I thought it sounded pretty good. All I needed now was to get hold of a guitar. I kept on attempting to stand, only to crash down again. I was hell bent on fighting this thing. I had no idea what it was, but I wasn't going to go quietly.

After a while, drained of energy but fortunately still breathing, I soon became aware of my emotions. Frustration and anxiety now piled into the mix. Fatigue overwhelmed me. I couldn't stand. The end point had arrived. Starting to see through the fog to see realism, never easy for a bloke like me, I unwillingly began to surrender to this new and frightening state I was in. More to the point, what were they going to do to me in hospital? Would they pump me full of something until I began to uncoil, the snake uncurling from dormant into sudden action? Whatever, I'd give it a go.

Mary called the ambulance. 999.

You might think at this point a wave of relief would sweep through me. It didn't. The problem I had was the thought of calling an ambulance made me feel that whatever was wrong with me, had beaten me. Stumped, done for. Heck, this was getting grave, a word with horrid connotations. Whatever it was, an ambulance meant a weighty, momentous episode. They would arrive, frown, then frown a bit more, a few quick tests, then deftly scoop me up from the floor, an out-of-control quivering wreck.

Two burly ambulance men arrived. Paramedics doing their routine thing but never once showing a blink of surprise. It was a comfort. They must have seen this hundreds of times before. I wasn't a freak, this was a common thing, a quick injection and I'd be back home tonight. Job done.

Onto the stretcher I went, lifted like a squashed old potato. It was then, being carried out of my flat, I was flooded by an emotional deluge. The laughter had gone. I wanted to curl up and cry.

Then came another little issue. Due to the design of the building, it was impossible to manoeuvre a stretcher through the front door. Forget the stretcher. Each of my arms were placed over a shoulder of each of the ambulance men as they took my weight. Clever chaps, these people. With luck, the doctors would be of the same mentality.

Mind you, I could sense their strain as they began to walk me out of my flat towards a waiting wheelchair. I was a lump.

By now, against my will, I was coming to terms with the real thing. What I was about to face wouldn't be a tea party. Emergency. Plonk. They wheeled me to the ambulance. No-one said very much. There wasn't much to say. Or laugh about. Something was wrong. I was a case. I was being rushed to hospital. Dear God.

The blaring two tone wail of the ambulance siren didn't help. I felt worse, more unsettled than ever. I was being rushed to hospital, and I didn't know what was wrong. An exploding mass of uncontrollable panic seized me as I battled to try and stop it.

The ambulance raced through the streets of London. SW11, my familiar stomping ground. I imagined all those drivers, bless them, moving to one side to allow the ambulance access in the congested streets. Polite, understanding, someone's life under threat, what if it happened to me, mount the pavement, let them through. By now I was practically hyperventilating, flat out on the stretcher. Sitting next to me was one of the ambulance crew. He offered me oxygen to breath from a mask, assuring me, in a calm and honest voice that it would help me relax. Thank God he was calm.

I had no idea then that my life was taking a new direction, one of self-discovery and positive change. Looking back, it was as if I had been abruptly woken from a deep sleep. But that was not how I felt then, hurtling through those London streets, terrified.

7

Climbing

I spent a gruelling two months in hospital, during which time I was eventually diagnosed with having Multiple Sclerosis (MS).

The words had horrible connotations. Wheelchair, crippled for life, dependency, carers, disabled. However, I had mixed feelings about this diagnosis. In one sense, it brought relief. A diagnosis, a name! I wasn't entirely mad. Others had been afflicted in the same way. Easy, I would be one of the crowd, new friends, a social life, great. But fear wouldn't allow me to be quite so jubilant. It hovered around me, frowning menacingly at my every move. I was frightened of the future and what it would mean…or not mean.

In hospital, I put on a brave face for my visitors. My emotions were far from stable and there was a wide gulf between how I felt, alone in the hospital, doing my best to cope, and greeting visitors. Sense of humour, man, keep it up, for their sakes if nothing else, laugh a bit, make them smile. You can cry when they've gone.

Another thing kicked in. Whilst dealing with my predicament I was also contemplating the loss of my brother a few months earlier as well as the progress of the police investigation. The shock, the anger, the loss, the terrible loss.

Then something happened. One day, on my first in-patient physiotherapy session, I felt weak. It was a combination of how it might feel being dunked in thick, sticky treacle, with that ghastly sensation of pins and needles. The session ended with me in a heap. Physically and emotionally, I felt done in. Flattened, rock bottom. I couldn't walk and could barely use my arms. I couldn't go on living like this. The future looked bleak, too bleak.

Grief from losing my brother swept over me then, a cold, unforgiving pool of numb, disorientating pain like I had never ever felt before. There was something hollow inside me, I could feel it, a gaping hole of nothingness, yet filled with an endless trail of miserable, heart-breaking sorrow. My hopeless situation hit me like a tonne of concrete landing on me. I began sobbing loudly, uncontrollably. My bruv, my friend, my best friend, one minute there, the next gone. A puff of wind. Shot down, dead.

This was followed by a profound sensation of being in a strange place. A mix of emotions took hold. I wanted so much to be strong, especially for my mom, and I was concerned for those visiting me who would see me with a long, wretched face. I was putting on a big bold brave face, suppressing my true feelings of helplessness and fear. The two were clashing, fighting each other, warring for peace, each as strong as the other.

Bit by bit, with the diagnosis, I began to accept my fate. The initial panic began to fade. I was on the go a bit too, travelling around. I was transferred from Chelsea & Westminster Hospital to Charring Cross Hospital and then back to Chelsea & Westminster and several visits to the National Hospital. Each hospital specialises in various testing such as CAT and MRI scans and blood tests and another neurological test. I was a traveller, this was fun. Anything to break the tedium, lift the gloom.

My specialist wanted to have a care plan put in place which included being allocated an adult social worker, occupational therapist, and care worker. It didn't sound all that great, but I went along with it. I would go along with anything to be honest.

Nonetheless, before the care plan was in place, I discharged myself back home, to my apartment in the sky. High rise. Up the stairs. This wasn't of much help and my specialist was keen to make sure I would be safe on my return home. 12 floors up.

And when you need a lift to function normally on an essential lift-must-work day, you can always, always, guarantee it won't. It will break down.

With superb timing, on the day of my return home, the lift decided to stop working.

The ambulance crew suggested taking me back to Chelsea & Westminster. I was having none of it. I wanted to be out of the hospital, home. I can do this. And I told them so.

I would go up on my backside while stabilising my upper body with one of my arms which was feeling less rubbery.

'I won't hold any of you liable,' I reassured the ambulance crew. Liable for what? I didn't want to think, pushing out the image of me tumbling down all 12 floors in a little roly poly ball.

'All you need to do is be there, one step after me, in case I tumble forward,' I said. A bit precarious but it I thought it sounded reasonably plausible.

They nodded and kindly obliged, agreeing to assist me on this mission. Phew, I was determined to get back home into my own space. There is nothing like home when you need it. And after a stay in hospital, you need home.

I was helped from my wheelchair and supported towards the steps to begin my journey up. A towering mountain was stretching above me. Steps, a lot of them, one at a time, you'll be ok. I hope.

One of them supported me under my right arm, my left arm holding onto the railing, and with one of my legs pushing better than the other. The other ambulance guy supported my upper body, guiding me upwards while helping to keep me stable. I needed that.

Take Your Marks…*Go!*

I wanted to rub my hands in glee. I was going to relish this upward challenge. It felt synonymous with a new path, a new life. Reckless, fired up. I tried not to think that a journey that used to take me less than three minutes to jog up, loving the exercise, now seemed like a hike up Mount Everest. Be quiet. That was the old life.

In hindsight, I now realise that being presented with 12 floors to climb was not a good idea just after coming out of hospital.

But at the time, I saw it as another test in the whole process. I was so relieved by the open-mindedness of the ambulance crew and our shared sense of adventure – an adventure! - to challenge the norm. I genuinely think that everything was meant to happen that way.

Over time however, my care plan in place, I eventually moved to a more suitable ground-floor flat. Much more sensible.

In hospital, I had learned that MS was an incurable disease that could destroy a sufferer, and that it is a condition that can manifest in multiple ways, and with no obvious external signs, mostly. Invisible! Thank God for that. Yet, at other times it can present itself as a noticeable, crippling, and devastating affliction. Push that one away, I would be the invisible sort.

In my body, MS manifested itself as a series of debilitating painful cramps, stiffness and paralysis of my limbs, loss of balance, muscle weakness, accompanied by severe pins and needles and visual instability. Wow. Sounded like a lot to digest. I had no idea at the time, when or if I would ever recover from this terrifying thing. Or if that would be possible, probably not. You're in for the long haul, mate, get used to it.

The condition can sometimes be responsible for making the sufferer appear as being lazy, clumsy, or even drunk. Never mind, think of all those times when I'd overdone the drink a bit, at least I would be used to that. These signs can be responsible for many errors in diagnosis and preconceived ideas of those looking on. Me, drunk? No, look, please, seriously, I have MS.

There was another thing too. On a psychological level, and depending on the lifestyle of the MS sufferer, someone afflicted with MS can become the target of resentment from the people with whom they come into daily contact. This was mainly due to a lack of knowledge and information that really should be available to employers, schools as well as the general public.

It is a disease that affects the central nervous system, causing destruction of the covering (myelin) of the nerve fibres in the brain and spinal cord. With MS, someone could be severely disabled one week, and appear perfectly normal the next.

Rather than dwelling on the intricacies of MS and becoming an expert on it, my past life experiences have taught me to be an expert of my own body.

Yet, in that ambulance, as it drove at high-speed, winding its way through the streets of London to get me to hospital, something happened, a change so profound it was to be the start of a healing journey that I could never have guessed would happen. The beginning of a realisation of what I had been doing to myself. While my internal dialogue had become a torrent of ominous questions, wondering if I were having a stroke or had I received one too many blows to my head when boxing, other thoughts were channelling through.

I was lucid enough to be clear in my mind that there was a connection between my bereavement, my response to it, and the sudden erosion of my health. It was too coincidental, too powerful to ignore.

Even writing this book is linked to the whole picture of everything that is contained within it, in more ways than one. A cathartic, emotive and enervating internal struggle, combined with peace…and yes, that hardest of words, forgiveness.

It was strange, and perhaps a medic might not be so ready to believe but even though I was experiencing inner turmoil and terrible physical immobility, somewhere, deeper inside, I was visited by a strong and conflicting awareness that convinced me that I was going to be alright. Everything was going to be fine. It was just my body, its loud, screaming, desperate message shouting at me: STOP WHAT YOU ARE DOING TO ME.

As the diagnosis of MS was given and I progressed through the system, I was beginning to understand the power to change the way how I looked at sickness, including other aspects of my life and the world in general. I could do better than this, I told myself. I didn't need to punish my body in the way I had been hell bent on doing, slowly stifling it. My body deserved better treatment, it was the only one I had, and it needed to be nurtured and looked after, not pummelled with a rod, battered to bits until it collapsed, defeated. I learned to use the power of choice, innate in us all, to relive a life of good health, happiness, and inner peace. I could get out of this mess. And I would.

Yet still my thoughts would bounce back to a physical cause. About a week before I had been taken to hospital, I had gone on a spontaneous, on the spur of the moment cycle ride. It was a round trip of approximately 70 miles, and I hadn't eaten anything that day. I had also drunk very little water and I was severely dehydrated. Could I have inflicted some internal damage that wasn't apparent at the time?

But even as I speculated, I knew I was still clutching at straws, desperate to find an answerer for my physical regression. I fought to move off this course, to stop contemplating which could only darken my thoughts. Just be patient and be calm, I said to myself instead. It wasn't easy.

But the thoughts kept repeating themselves over and over; I remember the end of my epic bike journey well, nearing my way home through the Battersea streets. The sun was low in the evening sky, and it was warm. I was pleased with myself for having ridden so far and I had returned safely. I had done well.

That golden sunset embraced me, and my breathing had slowed, when unexpectedly I fell off my bike and into the middle of the road. I hadn't anticipated how exhausted I had become. As I rolled over in the road and attempted to stand up quickly, so not to attract attention to myself, I was approached by two trendily dressed fresh faced teenagers.

As they ran to my aid one of them shouted, in a broad south London accent, 'Are you alright mate, do you need any help?'

Before I could say, 'No, thank you', one of them moved quickly in the direction of my bike and picked it up, the other helped me to my feet, I thanked them after they were satisfied that I was ok, and they walked away.

> *Doctors prescribe medicine of which they know little, to cure diseases of which they know less, in human beings of which they know nothing.'* Voltaire

Several days after that incident I decided to visit my GP, it was the second time in two weeks I had done this and knew that I needed a thorough check up.

Finding me in a doctor's surgery was a rare occurrence, but it had become clear to me that something just wasn't right. I needed to be sensible.

How could I fall off my bike like that? And why was it that on some days my limbs felt unusually heavy, as if I was dragging them through thick treacle? I had no idea then of what was to follow.

I was familiar with the term DOMS, which was an acronym for Delayed Onset Muscular Stiffness; this condition usually occurs after excessive exercise where the muscles become flooded with lactic acid. DOMS can cause stiffness and pain.

But what I was experiencing on that day was different; I struggled to make a comparison with anything I might have experienced during my past exercise exploits.

My second visit to the doctor confirmed some weakness in my muscles and now blurred vision in my right eye.

'Take these pain killers, twice a day,' was the doctor's advice, handing me a prescription.

I explained to my GP that it wasn't just any old pain that I was feeling. What I was experiencing was more like a sensation of numbness, an unexplained weakness.

I wouldn't take the pain killers anyway, I thought. I needed to stay in touch with the sensations that I was feeling, not mask them by painkillers. I understood enough to know that the pain was telling me that something wasn't right. Most of us have forgotten how to listen to our bodies and what they are trying to tell us. We think pain should simply be plastered over with pills, then we can forget all about it. And I didn't believe that pain killers wouldn't fix me. They would not treat the cause, only weakly attempt to hide the effect.

While observing the surreal reality of losing a loved one manifested itself, I had no idea that things could get any more surreal than they already were. Feeling that my life no longer belonged to me, it was as if I was suddenly trapped in a movie and my fate lay in the hands of the script writer and director. I was the puppet; the helpless actor moved around by the stranger above who held the strings.

In the meantime, there I was, lying in hospital, a wriggly little scrap. I had some use of my hands. I couldn't flap them around but at least I could wave a bit. The King does that, the Queen used to too. Great, put me on the balcony, give me a use, a job, I'll wave for you. On the downside, my left leg had given up; it had stubbornly decided to stop working. Nothing, zap. Blasted leg.

I thought about my GP, that saviour of all ills. We hope. Could he have protected me if I had been diagnosed sooner? Had I been a nincompoop? Whilst I will readily admit to that moniker best describing me at times, I concluded that, no, he couldn't. GPs are not God. They are what they are: general practitioners. They can only do as much as their training allows. Even for a chump like me. I needed God. Where the Hell had He gone? Disappeared behind a cloud, sunbathing.

8

Nurses

The days rushed by, they sometimes do in hospital, with the never-ending round of tests, blood samples, measuring, checking, chatting to fellow patients, changing this and that. After a while, I began to look forward to being allocated a wheelchair. A wheelchair! Sounded exciting. I wanted to move about, explore my new residence, and it would give me my independence back.

On one of my early explorations gadding about in my shiny new wheelchair, I discovered the room from where the hospital radio station was broadcasted. Aha, this was more like it. David would have been seriously impressed.

I befriended the presenter, always works to one's advantage. One day, I was invited on to one of his radio shows. Even better, on one occasion I was given the opportunity to present the show by introducing my selection of music. A DJ! Bring on the music. Wow, a dream come true. Me, a radio presenter! Bro' you're a star.

While sitting in the studio, happily churning out Marvin Gaye, Bob Marley, and Sam Cook, I was getting carried away, on a roll. I began to imagine I was entertaining the whole world, not just the patients in the hospital. I could picture David's drooling face. Hey, ho, I was having a great time, even if most of the patients were zonked out.

Until things slid downhill. After a few days, my condition took a turn for the worse. Instead of bringing me more independence, whizzing about the place on wheels, I was met with a block. I had been spending my days wheeling everywhere and anywhere. I would sometimes leave the hospital premises to take in a breath of traffic-fumed air. When you've found sudden freedom, exhaust-clogged air feels like a tonic. I loved it. David's face, watching me, would be a picture.

The trouble was, the excessive action of pushing the wheelchair with my weakening arms, caused them to lose about 90% of their strength. Things were not looking too good. Independence gone.

Initially the MS had mainly affected my legs, but now it had decided to progress upwards until eventually both my arms were reduced to lifeless rubber ropes. The power in my arms had suddenly switched off. They became void of feeling and sense. This was a disaster.

As the MS progressed further though my body, my right eye then decided to take on a life of its own; it was busy looking everywhere, except where I wanted it to. By now, I was in a meltdown of physical and mental disarray. I was frightened. I had no answers. I didn't think God did either.

After what seemed to be ages waiting, the result of the Magnetic Resonance Imaging (MRI) and the Computed Axial Tomography (CAT) scans were ready. The information gathered from the numerous neurological tests that I had taken previously was also now complete. When test results are due there is always that niggle. What's going to be revealed? Good, bad, or terrible.

The tests confirmed that MS was the cause of my body behaving the way it was. The early morning collapse, the falls while cycling. I'd ended up in a wheelchair in hospital, dreadful expression, it sounded like I'd ended up in a coffin. Nonetheless, I was still alive, and things were beginning to make some sense. Except, there was a 'but' that continued to swirl around in my mind. A big but.

On the upside, I felt a sense of relief at being told this diagnosis. I had needed to know exactly why my body was behaving the way it was. Now that I had a name to work with, in an odd way, that feeling I had of things getting better grew much stronger. Most people with a diagnosis of MS might sink in despair, a lifelong condition that could only get worse.

Contrary to this, I felt I had already reached my lowest point, it couldn't get much worse. From here, I could only go up.

Hospital was the place where I spent most of my time, challenging myself physically and mentally. Hah, there was still a bit of the tough dog in me. I wasn't finished yet. The problem with this strategy was that I kept tumbling off my bed or I would fold in a heap from my chair to the floor as I attempted to stand up or walk unaided. I experienced huge frustration in all my failed attempts, although there was plenty of amusement too. The nurses would look on patiently, maybe they'd seen it all before, it could only end in tears. I was naughty too, sometimes choosing not to play the perfect patient. I love being naughty. Boring, tedious, conforming to expectation, the model patient. They would find me flat on my back, often late in the evening, limbs flailing, looning around on the floor like a half-dead bottle fly on the window ledge.

A nurse would come running to my aid telling me off, while holding an empathetic gaze in her eyes. I refused to give up struggling to get back on my feet. Full marks for effort, man. It would have looked good on a school PE report. He tries.

I was blowed if I was going to accept disability, hence why I kept on attempting to force my body back into action. I simply could not ignore the call of my mind to get up and stand up, even when I knew that I would suffer the consequences after falling. Stubborn old mule, why couldn't he realise MS has no cure? Simple: I could not, and I would not.

Fortunately, my relationship with the nurses blossomed into a very good and amicable one. Over time we formed an understanding, and they became accustomed to my antics; there was a mutual respect between us, and we had fun. I appreciated this; it was a great help.

During the early weeks in hospital, I had managed to discover that no one knew the exact cause of MS. To me, this was positive. Some believed it was likely that it arose from a mixture of genetic and environmental factors. It seemed everything played a role.

I later found out that MS was a condition that would require drug treatments and physiotherapy, and it seemed to be diagnosed retrospectively. It could appear, whether you had experienced little or no disability for a period of 5, 10 to 15 years beforehand.

We get most of our vitamin D from exposure to sunlight, with low levels of vitamin D having been linked to higher numbers of people developing many different conditions, including MS. Contrary to this theory was the notion that MS sufferers were advised to avoid the sun. Funny old world.

I decided I would resist all medication. I wanted to keep my body clean of that. I did not want it clogged up with lotions and potions consisting of various chemicals that no-one really knew much about, much less about me. This was true Voltaire stuff, good on him.

As I continued with my resistance to any medicine, whatever it was, I recall a day when a friend of many years, called T, brought me infusions of herbs that were known to be good for the nerves; it was a concoction of St. John's Wort, vervain, ginger and more.

T was often affectionately called Herbal T. Accompanied by two acquaintances, he watched with enthusiasm as my eldest brother brought the cup to my lips. As I sipped the herbal nerve tonic, I simultaneously got the giggles which resulted with me beginning to choke. Blimey, heady stuff.

Some of the green-brown liquid brew found its way down my windpipe, and as I desperately gasped for air, T soon gave me several sharp blows to the middle of my back. Eventually, I caught my breath again, and the sound of tentative laughter filled the room at the spectacle of me choking on this sea-weedy concoction. A terrible way to go.

Initially, I had found with MS I seemed to easily choke on my food. I was not sure if my throat muscles were temporarily affected, as I don't remember this difficulty in swallowing lasting very long. Or perhaps it was my fear and anxiety receding.

My mom used to bring me blended homemade Jamaican-style fish soup while in the hospital, nutritious and tasty. Moms are good at this sort of thing.

On my request, when most of the ward was asleep, I remember two of the night nurses who would order one of my favourite dishes from the local takeaway, go on, please, please…Yes! Crispy duck and rice with black bean sauce. Naughty, but nice.

So fortunately, the MS did not adversely affect my appetite. I would eat practically everything, even having a pick at the hospital food now and again…now, that must mean being able to eat anything.

Then the following day, a good friend of mine called Abdul, who I had met during my college days, brought a book for me to read. It was called 'Notes from a Friend' by author and life coach Tony Robbins. Abdul and I had gone to see Anthony Robins several years before and we had had an amazing time. This book was a simple reminder that I, my thoughts and belief system were in control of my outcomes. So far, so good. This MS thing was not for me, nor was disability for life.

Every night before I fell asleep, I would imagine that I was in a boxing ring fighting something called MS. Phwooar, I would knock this one out flat alright, I was bigger and better than him, the silly weakling. Phwang! Zapp! Every night I would beat MS by knocking this ridiculous spectre right out of the ring. Stupid moron.

Slowly, over time, I noticed tiny impulses, like sparks of electricity, first in the little finger of my left hand, then gradually in other areas of my body. For me, and me alone, this was an indication that something good was happening. My body was slowly doing something positive in response to my own mental stimulation. Good on you, old boy, something is responding.

Initially, I decided to keep my minute progress to myself, I didn't want to run the risk of being ridiculed at this stage, and I had had enough of that already. I also had no wish to waste my energy fighting off non-believers. The doubters and the naysayers love to get a word in. Listen to the doctor, mate, take the pills.

I believed that these subtle movements in my body were indications that my healing was well under way, but I didn't think that everyone else would see it the same way; not that this mattered to me. My wobble bobble thinking refused to be deflated by medical experts, family, or friends. I was expert of my own body, no-one else, whatever books and manuals they had read, studied or exams they had taken. Only me knew me.

As I sat in the large hospital chair, I considered the feeling of strength and encouragement that I was experiencing from within. One day, from my hospital bed, I took note of a documentary that was showing on the ward television. It was about Mohamed Ali's battle with Parkinson's disease, and how he stood up to this crippling disease and would not give in. I drew inspiration from this and related to it in many ways.

A nurse entered the room asking me if I wanted to take a phone call; the voice on the other end of the line was official, yet friendly and familiar. It was the voice of Pat, the family police liaison officer. In my struggle and sudden descent into a different existence, I had never forgotten David, nor his cruel death.

'Hello, Mr. Hamilton,' she said. 'I'm sorry to disturb you, but I'm calling to inform you that the suspect is now in police custody.'

The news was a breath of fresh air. I permitted myself a smile. I felt this was an addition to the progress that I was having with my condition. Good news at last, I thought, and then I immediately wondered if they had really caught the right man.

Later I learned that his arrest was due to an anonymous tip-off, followed by a confession that had landed him in police custody. I was relieved, good.

9

The Storyteller

On my ward, there was a man who was in his senior years; he reminded me of the actor, Spencer Tracy. In the evenings, he would sit in a chair next to my bed and begin to tell a captivating story about a dog called Rex. In any other situation I would find this an odd gesture, but I was surprised at how these stories had a peaceful and therapeutic effect on my disposition.

While in hospital, I decided to utilise these stories and make them a part of my healing process since they gave me an unexplained sense of calm and optimism. A big thank you here to the comforter. It's often the simplest things in life that can bring the greatest reward.

As the female registrar placed the stethoscope on my chest to listen to my breathing and heartbeat, she asked in a soft friendly voice, 'How are you today, Mr. Hamilton?'

She was young with a kind face and a subtle smile, and I didn't give her an immediate answer.

My eyes were fixed on the small portable television in the corner of the room I was now in. What I was seeing reinforced my surreal existence. It was a news flash. The Twin Towers in New York were crashing down to the ground.

As I stared at the television behind her, the registrar followed my eyes and turned to look in the same direction to see what had captured my attention. I felt her sudden tight squeeze on my hand, and as she turned her head in my direction again, I could see her eyes filling with tears and disbelief. What was going on?

The images on the TV that terrible day were overwhelming, almost unbelievable, yet indicative of a horrible truth; we both watched in silence as the drama unfolded, the date was September 11th, 2001.

Initially, my mind played tricks. I was expecting Bruce Willis to appear and come running to the rescue, but he never did. This was real. We had only just crept into the 21st century. Was this the future? More violent, more ruthless...more hate-filled? No room for a word called forgiveness...and certainly not from Al Quaeda.

One day I was lying on my hospital bed ready and waiting for another session of physiotherapy. As I lay there, I recalled what I had read about hospital patients becoming emotionally dependant to their institution. Was this me? Was I enjoying myself a bit too much? Easy camaraderie with nurses and patients, visits by mum, sneaky takeaways, the dormitory schoolboy.

Shortly after this, thoughts of the outside world began, unexpectedly, to rush through my head. A slight panic, a feeling of being trapped. Where were the emergency exits? How would I evacuate safely from the hospital if the worst was to happen? What if the terrorists bombed this place? There's always a What if... in most of us. But mine took on a scary reality. My vulnerability loomed large.

On my return from the physiotherapy session, I wasn't feeling too good, emotionally rather than physically. I started to reflect on how independent I use to be. A world away from this. Now, I needed help just to change my clothes. Not only that, the worst thing of all: I began feeling sorry for myself.

I had been based on a transit ward, a temporary stopgap before being allocated a long-term ward. My thoughts were abruptly disturbed by the sound of two nurses who had begun to prepare a vacant bed next to mine. My bed had to be moved a little to make space for it with all the accompanying equipment for the new admission. Several minutes later, I noticed someone being wheeled in on a hospital trolley by the porters, and then carefully placed in the vacant bed. I glanced across at the patient as he was being wheeled in, thinking how his situation appeared more physically challenging than mine.

The newcomer was a young man in his late twenties to early thirties. His head looked up to the ceiling, just staring. He never turned his head; his hair was dark and short, and there was a small area at the front which was a striking silvery grey. He looked barely alive.

When he first spoke, I felt he needed to talk; his voice sounded cracked, anxious, a quick pace...nervous, maybe he was in shock, I thought. Or maybe I was.

Without turning his head, he sensed my presence. 'Hi,' he called out in a friendly voice.

'Hi,' I responded. At least he could talk.

In a quiet, strained voice the man continued, 'My hair went grey after the accident, I think I'm fucked.'

I looked at him and didn't answer, I didn't know what to say. I didn't want to disturb him by getting him to talk too much,

'What's wrong with you then?' he asked, sounding mildly confident. A voice that had clearly once commanded authority.

'Been diagnosed with MS,' I told him.

'Ah, so sorry, that doesn't sound too good.'

'What about you?' I asked him. 'An accident, you say. What happened?'

His reply was devastating to say the least.

'I was out playing rugby,' the man, whose name was Paul, said. 'Having my usual Saturday morning fun with the team. Love it. Fresh air, exercise, can't beat it.' For a tiny moment, he had sounded excited. Then his voice changed. 'There was a scrum, and I was in the front,' he said. 'When the ball was thrown in, the scrum collapsed.'

I stared across at him, waiting for him to go on.

'The last thing I remember,' he said, 'was seeing the green grass in close focus and the boots, socks and calves of my fellow rugby players.'

I continued to look at him.

'The next thing was I regained consciousness and discovered I was in hospital having scans and Xray's.'

It was difficult to know what to say, a banal, 'I'm sorry to hear that' or 'Dear God, sounds awful, mate.' 'Bad luck, old chap.'

'My neck had been broken,' he said, and added quietly, 'I'll never walk again, much less play rugby.'

I stared at him, utterly lost for words. There was nothing I could say that could possibly help, not even light humour. 'Look on the bright side, mate, always someone worse off.' 'Hah, you're alive, that's what counts.' Alive! Who would want that? My predicament paled into insignificance, compared to his fate. I felt suddenly selfish, self-centred, mucking about with the nurses, midnight feasts, a laugh a day.

'Stupid thing is,' he went on, filling the silence. 'It's a bit ironic. I am – or let's say, I was – a young policeman. I had my career ahead of me.'

I shook my head, filled with a wringing mixture of emotions at his predicament, almost disbelief. What on earth was he going to do with the rest of his life.

'Stupid thing is,' he said. 'My job would sometimes involve chasing criminals over hazardous terrain.' He paused and took a breath. 'Dodgy garage roofs, derelict buildings, broken windows, rickety tiles, you name it, I've climbed over it.' He let out another breath, almost a sigh. 'Then to go out like this...playing rugby, enjoying my favour...'

Paul didn't complete his sentence. His words had fallen silent. Then I could hear the sobbing and snivelling. I had no words of comfort, nothing that could come anywhere close to relieving his pain. I wanted to cry too.

His words echoed in my mind, chasing criminals over perilous terrain only to break his back playing the game he loved.

'Be strong,' was all I could say. 'Just be strong.'

Several hours later my armchair-styled wheelchair taxi arrived to take me for more tests.... that was the last time I saw Paul.

I will never know what happened to him or how he coped with his life after that, but I never forgot him.

My stay in hospital brought me into contact with some very special people. For some, this reality and time was coming to an end. However, I was honoured to have been in the company of many of them. Mrs. Campbell was no exception,

'Hello, dear!' she had greeted me cheerily. She was a patient who had come down from the cardiology ward to visit me.

'Are you the one who is refusing medication?' she asked. Mrs. Campbell was a lively, Jamaican woman in her mid to late sixties who claimed to have lived life to the full and had given birth to 12 children.

I nodded. 'Yes, that's me.'

We had met a couple of days previously. She was one of those warm, affectionate ladies you cannot help instantly liking.

'You should take your medicine, you know,' she said. 'It is good for you. It will make you better.'

I smiled at her. 'I'm doing fine,' I said. 'I feel I am doing the right thing by not taking medication.'

She frowned.

I told her what I had already informed the ward nurse and

registrar. 'If my body has put me like this,' I said. 'Then it is for a reason. I believe my body will repair itself over time.'

She shook her head. I could not help noticing the obvious disapproval written all over her face.

'If I was to ingest a synthetic medicine,' I went on. 'Then my body would become confused. My natural healing process would be adversely affected.'

The darker expression on Mrs. Campbell's face suddenly cleared. To my surprise, she then said, with conviction, 'You know something? You're right. I'm not going to take my medicine either.'

'No, no Mrs. Campbell,' I protested. 'You can't stop taking your medication just like that, you need to consult your medical team and inform them of your intensions, then discuss with them the pros and cons.'

She gave me a quizzical look.

'Your body is now dependent on the medicine that you are taking,' I told her. 'I wouldn't advise that you just stop taking your pills.'

With a wide, crooked, and mischievous grin, Mrs. Campbell said, 'You're right, you know, yes, you're right!'

We both laughed and chatted together about her life and mine; she talked about her childhood in Jamaica and the fun that she used to have growing up there. It sounded idyllic. From that day on, Mrs Campbell and I would visit each other to chat about the weather and current affairs, breaking up the monotony of our clinical surroundings.

Then one day, not long after this exchange, when the hazy rays of the autumn sun were streaming through the hospital windows, a nurse whose name was Grace approached me. She was aware that I was a friend of Mrs Campbell.

As I struggled to adjust my upper body in the chair that I was sitting in, I couldn't help but noticing the solemn look in her eyes.

'Hello,' Grace said. 'I thought you might want to know that Mrs.

Campbell died this morning.' She looked at me with genuine sadness in her eyes, even though as a nurse she would have encountered death thousands of times. 'I'm so sorry.'

10

Bad Nurse

Some people do jobs that they love, and some people do jobs that they hate, money being the only motivation. One late night as I lay in my bed drowsing, I noticed that the night nurse had begun her duties.

In the dim lights of the hospital ward, I could see that this wasn't our usual nurse; the outline of her stature and her ridged movements were different and unfamiliar. As she approached my bed, I gently closed my eyes. Unexpectedly, I felt someone prodding me, and rather too brutally for comfort, with what seemed like a hard wooden stick. The night nurse usually gave out the night-time medication after coming on duty before patients settled down for the night.

Didn't she read the notes at the foot of my bed, I thought? It clearly stated that I wasn't on any medication, so why was she attempting to attract my attention with such force and enthusiasm? I didn't like it. It didn't feel right or appropriate. It certainly did not seem the sort of movement anyone would expect form a nurse in hospital, there to take care of you.

Eventually, I opened my eyes and looked up to see a stony face looking down at me; her eyes looked angry. She seemed startled by my sudden alertness. It was late at night, and I suddenly felt vulnerable. Staring directly into her eyes, I told her never to put her hands on me like that again while working on this ward. I think she might have been startled that a patient could speak to her like this, putting her in her place. There was no answer and she quietly retreated into the shadows of the ward.

The following morning, after I made an official complaint about my experience with the night nurse, it was revealed to me that several other complaints had been made by patients about the same nurse. I was assured that the nurse would not be returning to this hospital. Fortunately, that experience was an isolated one; all the other nurses who looked after me were kind, friendly and good-natured. This was a person who liked to be in control, and she must have been doing this before to those weaker than herself, getting away with it because many patients, especially the elderly, do not complain or feel to worried that if they complain, they will be marked out and punished. However, the incident demonstrated the importance of speaking out in such circumstances, however physically or emotionally vulnerable you may feel.

I continued to learn as much as I could about my illness; I would use what I had learned to help me to appease my condition, hence regain my independence, wellbeing, and my life. I believed that the knowledge and understanding of the human mind and body, which I had gained over the years, would help me to overcome my debilitating existence. Mind and body are inextricably linked. The messages you feed your body can be revealing.

Consciously, I decided to put my mind in a state of abeyance, a temporary denial of the issues relating to the disease. I intended to challenge my new health condition from a different viewpoint. Aware of the continued research to find a cure for MS, and, crucially, how some people with MS had discovered alternative and natural solutions to helping their condition. I had listened to, and read, their stories with growing interest.

Now, here I was, one of those people who had chosen the alternative and natural path to regaining their health, drawing on the body's own inbuilt self-healing mechanism. Having learnt about my story up to this point, now is the time for me tell you how I did it and how I arrived at where I am now. This is not a manual on self-healing to persuade any one of you to follow, nor is it meant to carry a persuasive message for you to stop a current path of healing or medication and switch over to what I did. It is meant solely for your interest and perhaps to inspire you with hope. There can be another way.

When I observed my MS symptoms, I was convinced that however appalling and negative, my symptoms were the result of collective negative thoughts, an acidic diet, and the wrong type of exercise. A healthily operating body, I reasoned, would give way to a healthy mind, and vice versa.

Acutely embittered by the events of the past and my brother's death, I wanted to attempt to restore balance though physical exercise, without it being excessive, and a healthy diet. How could the body descend into a physical wreck if all else was in place in the right balance of diet and positive thinking?

The combination of negative thinking with a diet of acid foods had added to doing too much exercise and produced even more acidic waste in my blood in the form of lactic acid. This toxic combination had eventually resulted in my body shutting down. Was it surprising, I asked myself?

My body had become a soup of acids, and it was not a very appetising soup. It was detrimental to my health. Like a domino effect, the health of my body affected my emotions, and my emotions affected the health of my entire body. The two were like hand in glove.

11

Forgive?

I learnt that one of the first lessons during the healing process was learning how to forgive. I swallowed in a gulp. Forgiveness was going to be a tough one for me to face. Someone out there had committed the brutal act of a senseless murder of my brother, shooting him at close range. He had stood no chance and now he had gone, obliterated from life; his future had stretched ahead of him, whilst this man still walked and lived, enjoying his existence, even if he was in prison. How and why should I forgive? Never mind, old chap, I know you didn't really mean it, a slip of the fingers, it's fine. It wasn't fine and yet, deep down, I already knew the answer. Did he regret what he had done? Had he now stopped to consider the effects of his actions? Did he have a side to tell? Was he suppressing what had happened, hoping it would go away? Or did he feel profound guilt, an equally toxic item to hold within your mind? Forgiving did not mean that I should be feeling sorry for him, sympathising with his predicament but it did mean I had to clear my body of hate and revenge.

Forgiving this person was the price that I had to pay for regaining my health, it was as simple as that. I needed to learn how to honestly forgive the soul who took the life of my brother, and I needed to forgive myself too. I needed to be kind to myself, instead of whacking my body with a punishment I did not deserve.

I understood how my destructive, yet justified emotion of retribution, could only lead me to self-destruction. And I had already pressed that button, banging on it with all my strength. There was no lower level I could sink to. Like an elevator that has reached the ground floor, I had to begin to rise again. After all, in this sunken state, I was effectively fuelling a greater triumph in the murderer. He may be languishing in prison, but he had his health and mobility. I, on the other hand, was languishing in a different prison and with less freedom. I had been punishing myself, I had a different bullet lodged in my head, self-inflicted.

I could not afford to feel sorry for myself either; I could not give in to this enemy that was ravaging my body. Instead, my mental energies were increasingly being used as fuel for my determined efforts to get up and walk again.

Throughout my life I have heard people speak of forgiveness, mainly from a biblical or religious perspective. But what I had discovered now was that forgiving was a tool for healing. It would become the prerequisite to my process of self-healing for my body and mind.

This was easier said than done. It was not going to happen overnight.

Enduring the pain of losing my brother at the hands of a cold-hearted killer, had caused me to question the meaning of forgiveness and revenge. One of these elements is a healthy emotion, one is highly toxic.

I had a choice to make. Either I continued to submerge myself in this grimy cocktail of acidic emotions which would eventually slowly poison me from within, and the only person getting hurt, was me.

Or I could choose to forgive. Forgiving can be like the letting go of a heavy poisonous load. Once thrown away, it will make space. The space must be filled by something, it cannot simply be left empty. This was going to be essential for true healing of the mind, body, and soul.

Forgiveness is like disowning an acidic gift and returning it to the sender with unconditional love. When you allow that space to fill up with something else, you can fill it with enlightening, uplifting, good things. You can feel energy pounding through from deep inside where it counts. Hate, on the other hand, is a very strong word. Listen, as you go about your daily life, and you will hear it being used freely in many different circumstances. It is energy draining, a futile waste, a bitter, reckless emotion that ferments, pooling in every fibre, every sinew and cell of your mind, seeping with relentless vigour into your blood, your physical being. I had been consumed with hate. I had made it my friend, there to turn to whenever I needed to lean on it. I leaned on it every single day. I could have glugged it down from a self-filling tumbler.

I know all too well, how easy it is to hate someone who has caused you great pain and sadness, and how difficult it is to forgive them, much less show them love. It takes a great deal of courage.

Forgiving carries a bundle of free, super-powered energy. It thrives on wellbeing and an 'all's good with the world' feeling. A contentment that fills into every cavity of your body, mind, and soul. It is a great and powerful gift to be able to send thoughts of love to those who have caused you harm. The same is true of yourself. Forgiveness wings its way back to you like a boomerang.

Think of it as being a bit of an alchemist, working with bundles of thoughts and emotions. Instead of turning bottles and jars of ordinary liquid metals into gold, negative thoughts and energies are transmuted into positive and constructive ones. Often in equal measure.

Did I meet David's killer and forgive him face to face? No, is the simple answer. I did not. I did not get that chance. I was informed that he was extradited to stand trial for two other suspected murder charges in his country of birth. Would I have done, given the chance? Possibly, but probably not. This was not because I did not believe I could go that far. It was because at this stage of my forgiving process, I had an innate conviction that I did not need to see the perpetrator in the flesh to truly forgive them and decided it did not really matter.

Forgiveness is about the energy, good or bad, that we send out to each other. Whatever we send out in thought form does come back in some way. Whether that is positive or negative. And if it is negative, I do not think there is anything to fear. It will lead to taking another step, another way forward that you may come to look back upon later and realise it was meant, perhaps to have a more positive effect in another way.

Carrying a sack full of resentment, revenge and bitter, hateful thoughts is a huge, load. What sort of strain does that cause on your back, shoulders, neck, your entire internal system? Forgiveness is like letting go of a heavy weight you have been lugging around on your shoulders and returning it to where it belongs. The flow of energy goes out and it cannot be destroyed, it has to land somewhere but it won't boomerang back onto you. Telepathic thought works in a parallel. Good or bad thoughts, it is your choice which one you send out and what effect that has on your health.

I have discovered the profound benefits gained from this fresh approach to life, and this way of thinking can propel my mind to a place of inner peace when required, which in turn energises my body. It is indescribable, an experience which transcends all else. It takes time and these things cannot be rushed. You must be patient.

I have since discovered that here are reports based on experiments where athletes have excelled in athletic events when they have held in their mind thoughts of love. Love is the direct opposite of hate. Wouldn't you rather live with good health and energy, than in a pit of murky liquid, clogging up the myriad pathways within you?

The Japanese scientist, businessman and author, Dr Masaru Emoto, who has published several volumes of a work, one entitled, Messages from Water, carried out a variety of frozen water experiments. This is where he observed the frozen water crystals under a microscope.

The experiments carried out by Dr Masaru Emoto showed that when phrases such as 'love, appreciation' and 'thank you' were written and placed on glasses of water before freezing, it was reported to have caused the frozen water to form beautiful, geometrical crystals.

On the other hand, it was observed where phrases such as 'you make me sick', or 'I hate you' would produce frozen water crystals that were like that of polluted water.

Dr. Emoto concluded that our thoughts and mind can have a profound effect on our physical wellbeing.

You can find details of these experiments here:

Japanese Water Crystal Experiments | eHow.com: http://www.ehow.com/list_7445940_japanese-water-crystal-experiments.html#ixzz1rf1TM3qi

As far as my treatment was concerned, I had two options open to me. Option one was to be acquiescent and take up the offer of pharmaceutical drugs. Option two meant that I could follow a silent whisper inside me that was instructing me about the things that I needed to do to find true healing.

When I listened, I could hear my body telling me what I needed to eat, what exercises I need to do and how I needed to think. Then I would seek out the relevant foods and books that would support my ideas.

Over the years, I had discovered that there are many natural healing and alternative medicines that are serving people around the world to liberate themselves from devastating afflictions. I have discovered that we were born with our own unique natural power, a 'Natural Blueprint' that our body uses to heal itself. I felt that pills and medication would block this, suppressing it back.

I learnt about the power of cleansing my body on the inside, and how critically important this process is. Good nutrition was imperative to my wellbeing, and I discovered there is a mass of evidence that substantiates all of this.

In today's world you can find many types of physical exercise regimes. However, in my search for alternative approaches to my health, I discovered how a particular holistic type of exercise would lead to an all-round deeper level of health.

A mind crammed with fear, anger, and worry, together with a poor diet, will lead to disease and ill health. It is inevitable.

But what is even more significant is the evidence that demonstrates how the mind can also assist with the actual healing of the body.

What I endeavoured to do became more and more clear. I would combine positive thinking with a diet of wholesome, alkalising foods and holistic exercise. I would begin to produce more energy than I lost.

Because I changed my mind set and my belief system relating to my health, I was able to free myself from the devastating clutches of MS. I have experienced that when you dare to think outside the box, the incredible happens.

The moment that I began to question my beliefs and alter my mindset, new and relevant information relating to health began to appear in my life.

12

Limiting Beliefs

It was only due to my childhood conditioning that I formed limiting beliefs that related to my life and to my health.

These beliefs were based on fear, and I grew up believing that I was not responsible for my illnesses, and that the solutions lay outside of my control. I grew to accept that it was other people who knew what was best for me when I was unwell.

> At a young age, the elephant is chained to a post. The chain is strong, and it prevents the baby elephant from escaping; every time the baby elephant tries to break the chain, it cannot.
>
> The elephant's Strength and Will are worn down and squashed. Then, as the elephant grows up, it forever remembers that it was unable to break free from the chain, and therefore never tries to break free.

The original author of this story is unknown, but the message is a powerful one. Even though it would take almost zero effort for that elephant to break the baby-sized chain, it identifies so strongly with the past that it cannot see the present reality of how strong it really is. Instead, it will give up, telling itself it doesn't have the kind of strength needed.

It was more than forty years ago when I had the experience of learning that there existed an alternative approach to my health. I was in my early teens and returning home from a visit to the local GP, clutching some medicine he had prescribed me for a painful knee.

Fortunately for me, I was spotted by Denise, a much older woman who was a neighbour that lived several doors away from me. She was in her late thirties, attractive, kind, and inquisitive.

'Where're you coming from then?' she inquired kindly.

I explained to Denise that because of a pain in my knee from playing rugby I went to the doctor, and he gave me these pills to take.

Denise asked if she could have a look at what I had been prescribed by my GP. I handed her the paper packet and as she read the label of the medicine inside, I noticed her facial expressions painted a picture of anger and distress. She developed an irritated and disappointed aura. In a concerned, motherly sort of way, Denise asked me if I wanted to meet a friend of hers who just so happened to be a medical doctor.

'He's in my house now, and he could give you more information on this drug', she informed me.

I walked with Denise up the hill past my house and towards hers, grasping the paper bag in which was my so-called medicine.

Sitting in the lounge was a middle-aged man wearing glasses and slightly bald.

'Hi Tom,' Denise said, 'This is Garry, my friend and neighbour, he has some medicine that I want you to have a look at.'

As Denise invited me to sit down, she offered me a soft drink. Tom reached out and took the pharmaceutical package from my hand. After inspecting the label, Tom convincingly and confidently advised me to 'flush this poison down the toilet immediately.'

He went on to explain that 'this medicine is given as a muscle relaxant but has the potential of creating a barrage of dangerous side effects in the body, and that I shouldn't take them. I never did take that medicine and my knee corrected itself over time. Several decades later that same knee has never given me trouble again.

When I was initially diagnosed with MS, in the beginning I did not have a concrete reason as to why I did not want to take any pharmaceutical drugs. My decisions at the time could have been based on instinct, and gut feeling influenced from my past as well as having people in my life like Denise, just at the right time.

13

Healing Regimes

While I was in hospital, my stubborn stance caused some frustration amongst family members, medical staff, and friends alike, but my mind was already made up.

The explanation that I would give to those who dared to enquired about my abstinence from conventional medicine, was that if my body put me like this then my body could make me better. This was my new mantra and I believed it one hundred percent.

My reasoning was that my body's natural healing process needed to be left alone to do its own thing, and not be put in a state of confusion with manmade drugs. What has been so encouraging for me is that since that year 2001 and the time when this book was revised in December 2022, I continue to live a relatively normal life, MS free.

During this time, I have uncovered a torrent of information relating to alternative health that confirms my initial gut feelings. Back in 2001 my mind was made up and I chose to use my body as my own personal human guinea pig, experimenting with alternative therapies, diets, remedies and exercise.

Over time, I discovered what food stuffs were beneficial for me, and I was slowly beginning to reclaim an improved quality of life for which I will forever be grateful. With every decision that I have taken in life, and whether the outcomes have been perceived as good or bad, I realise that there is a lesson to be learned from the outcome.

This true story is no different because it emerged from where the life of my brother ended, and as a tribute to him, I am sharing it with you. Without David's death from that gunshot, I might never have discovered this rich new path in my life. It almost feels like a gift sent from him to place a meaning on his death, to help me escape the vicious cycle of untamed hate and anger that had consumed me.

Experiencing that personal power involves living, in the now, in the present, and by being in the here and now I was able to break the chains of my past and embark on an amazing journey of synchronicity, healing, and self-discovery.

As well as my lesson in forgiveness, I learned to trust and surrender to the great power of love. Not the romantic love between two people, but the unconditional love that exists between me and all human beings.

If you wake up in the morning and you feel aches and pains, then you know you are alive. However, your body is trying to give you a message. Something isn't right and needs attention. The body is excellent at doing this, it will always do its best to keep you healthy and safe.

I was lying on my back in a green field, and at my head stood a Native American male. At my feet on her knees, was a female of the same tribe. The male had a spear that seemed to be piercing my chest; I was not alarmed as I instinctively felt that he was drawing off negative energy from my heart.

The Native American woman was holding the palms of her

hands against the soles of my feet; I could feel that she was giving me healing energy and it was good.

When I woke from this dream, my senses were hazy; I noticed that the hospital ward lights had been toned down; it must be after mid-night, I thought.

Then suddenly, I was thrown into a state of panic, not because of the familiar feelings of pain and lifelessness of my limbs, but by a new challenge that had visited me in the night.

As I breathed out, I was convinced that I was unable to breathe in; I was grasping for air, and my windpipe felt as if it was shrinking. My immediate thought was that this must be a panic attack.

My chest continued to feel heavy, and my windpipe felt constricted; I was suffocating, and I began to panic; in my head I was screaming out for help.

Then, in the dim of the hospital lights, I noticed a figure standing beside my bed; it must be the night nurse because she took my hand and held it in hers close to her chest. I could feel her warmth and the moment that my hand was taken I could feel calm. I felt safe as she softly stroked my forehead, whispering everything will be alright. I fell asleep.

In the morning, Royston, a kind-hearted hospital auxiliary, revealed to everyone on my ward that it was his last shift, and that he would soon be off to America. As he left the ward, he exclaimed, 'Oh, I have something for you!'

When he returned, Royston gave me an envelope, and in it was a card; it was a reproduction old black and white photograph of Chief Joseph, a famous Native American Chief.

On the back of the card, Royston had written these words:

'Garry, please continue to shine like the sun and be an inspiration to all who have the privilege of crossing your path. Like day will surely turn to night, all that follows is how it should be. Continue to be free.' Royston.

The words on the card made me think about my dream with the

Native Americans giving me healing, and I wondered in awe about the synchronicities of life and the coincidences that we sometimes take for granted.

I was waiting patiently in the bulky hospital chair that had four small wheels for the easy transference of patients. It wasn't exactly a wheelchair, more like an armchair on wheels.

Unexpectedly, a thought entered my mind, and I remembered the time when I was invited to watch a football match. It was my first ever live professional soccer match. I recall that it was an England Cameroon friendly, and I was freezing cold.

What I found fascinating at the time though, wasn't exactly the match itself, but it was the way my brain was reacting. First, I noticed how every player, including the ball looked so tiny compared to seeing them on the TV.

But what was interesting was how I expected my eyes to refocus and to zoom in on the action, slow motion replays and all, just as it happens when watching football on TV.

This visual experience reminded of the significance of looking at reality with my own eyes and not through eyes whose vision is distorted by preconceptions and slanted viewpoints. As I would soon be leaving hospital I began to reflect on my experiences, including some of the characters who I'd met during my time there. I thought of the Welsh man, Harry Jenkins, who also had MS. He came to the hospital for a vaccination to make him walk again.

Through boredom maybe, Harry and I decided to bet on each other based on who would be the first one to stand up and hobble across the floor of the ward to the other side of the room we were in. The competition began on the day Harry took his vaccination, I was told that his medication would take effect within a few days, so I didn't have long to get myself moving.

It was with tremendous strain, struggle, falling over and barely finding my balance, that on the sixth day after Harry took his jab, I managed to shuffle to the other end of the room, unaided. As the winner, even though I collapsed in a heap and needed the help of the nurses again to get me to my chair, Harry congratulated me, and we chuckled.

Harry then confided in me that his wife was always telling him to take alternative remedies, but he had always been against it. He said to me, 'I've been taking this steroid vaccine for a long time now, and it doesn't have the same positive effect on my body as it once did.'

On the day of my discharge from hospital, my main registrar asked me if he could at least offer me an aspirin. I think he must have felt a little powerless that I refused medication and that he could not help me further. We both chuckled as I shook my head and told him, 'No thank you.'

Earlier during my hospital stay, my medical registrar had asked me if I would be interested in meeting someone from my ethnic background who had this MS condition and had been successfully treated at the hospital.

As I had been keen to meet this individual, I then reminded the registrar that I never did meet his former MS patient as he had recommended by him.

His smiling face became rigid with cold, and a steely like professionalism. He then informed me, 'He had lost the former patient from their data base.'

We proceeded to shake hands and I thanked him for all he had done. I was wheeled along the long corridors to the lift that took us to the ground floor level where the ambulance was waiting.

I was going home at last. I had succeeded, I thought. Although I was treated well at the hospitals, and I had more pleasant memories than unpleasant ones, I was still looking forward to going home.

However, I still wondered what had happened to that former patient who had been recommended to me as a good example in the treatment of MS with pharmaceutical drugs. Had he lived? Had he got worse over time? Had a relapse? Or was he playing basketball, football, living an active life? I somehow doubted it.

My stay had lasted 2 months, and I had not become institutionalised. I wanted to go home where I would begin my quest for further good health and wellbeing.

At home, I thought about some of the most interesting and beautiful people that I had met in hospital. It had been an inspiring experience and I had learnt from all of them. I recalled the nurses, Mrs. Campbell, the storyteller, Royston, the rugby player the list went on.

At home, I was, however, free. I could roll about on the floor as much as I wished, I could crawl to the kitchen or bathroom, I could experiment and test myself without a concerned nurse rushing to my aid in case I hurt myself. I never resented the nurses for coming to help me, they were doing their job and were a constant reassurance. Sometimes I missed their attention, but I also knew that I had to retrain my brain and I would need to do this alone. I had to relearn the hard way. When you allow your body to use its own healing power, rather than lean on possibly quick-fix medication, it often does take hard work.

I continued with a hand exercise that I used to do whilst in hospital as it was something that I learned in my youth and would become my barometer informing me when my condition was improving.

I would hold my index and the middle finger of each hand together and do the same with the little and ring finger.

Then, forming a V-sign like an alien salute, I would open and close them together again. Sometimes, I would vary the movements by isolating different fingers and move just the index or little finger alone. The more I could select which finger to isolate the better I felt because I could see the physical result that told me my body was healing.

As I retrained my body, I began to understand that to promote healing in my life it would need to be done holistically, mind and body. These changes would include the food that I ate, what I chose to drink, the type of exercises I would do and, crucially, my thoughts.

My brother's death continued to be a part of my thoughts, but this was now on a more analytical basis, rather than hate filled. As my healing progressed, I learned the official reasons why my brother was killed. Many months had gone by since he had once trusted a stranger who had begged him for leniency. This stranger had collided with my brother's car whilst on his mobile phone, and had begged my brother, due to lack of insurance, to settle the damages privately. The months of delay in settling this verbal agreement, the unreturned telephone messages and subsequent frustrations rolled on. It was an eventual chance meeting between them both which led to an angry exchange and my brother was shot in the heart. His friend who he was with was also shot and killed. Madness.

My healing regimes began. I decided I would choose what I wanted to experience. Like a projector, I could use my thoughts to project onto a mental imaginary screen the images of those thoughts, and which I chose to experience.

I refused to dwell for too long on past traumas and events and began to utilise positive visualisation by always seeing myself walking again in the warm sunshine.

By now, my mind was flooded with material from books on healing with the mind and subjects such as Neuro Linguistic Programming (NLP).

I recalled reading about how basketball players, gymnasts, and athletes in general would use visualisation techniques to enhance their physical performance, and with great success, and these techniques could also work for certain disabilities.

To condition my body as well, physical exercise was important as well as training my mind to think in a new and powerful way. At this point I was familiar with many types of western type exercises and stretch routines. However, I was now looking for something different, something that was internal that would strengthen me from within.

Internal martial arts, more specifically Tai Chi and Chi Kung, became my choice of daily exercise. Over several weeks of practice, the subtle movements in my little fingers grew into more obvious ones. The movement in my toes too, were becoming more apparent and my confidence was cautiously growing larger. Within two months I was able to use a walking frame to go to go to the local shops.

While on one of my shopping trips, I passed a used book shop that I had never been into before. Outside, I inadvertently noticed a book poking out from under a larger pile of books. I pulled the barely visible paperback from under the pile, and I was energised by just reading its title, 'The Art of Chi Kung'.

This remarkable book contained special and relevant information that I had longed to read and was delighted to have it in my possession. At home I began to read this amazing book; I was unable to put it down, and when I felt ready, I carefully studied the pages before eventually practicing one of the exercises.

I am not claiming that the information in this book is a cure, but all I can say is that I felt different, more solid and balanced than I had felt since the retreat of my health. There was no way this could have been a placebo effect. It was genuine natural healing. I practiced only one specific Chi Kung exercise and it proved more beneficial than I expected. I was amazed, the bug had bitten me.

In short, Chi Kung refers to the ancient Chinese practices of accumulating Chi, or energy, within the body. In Chinese, the words Chi (or Qi) means air, life force or dynamic energy, and Kung (or Gong) means work. Chi Kung is a type of exercise that involves slow gentle movements or even being motionless and calm with rhythmic breathing, there are many different types of Chi Kung.

Qi is circulated throughout the body and permeates every part of it, keeping each cell alive. This in turn benefits the heart, lungs, kidney, and digestion by balancing the amount and the circulation of Qi in the body. It is very easy to learn, most people will be able to execute the basic movements within a short time. However, mastering the finer and more subtle points may take much longer. Patience is required.

I joined one class that was run by a renowned master of the art. After my first lesson I continued to be surprised at how energised I was feeling, and I noticed that my frame of mind was calmer. Over the months people who knew me could see definite improvements in my movements and general coordination. My muscles felt stronger, my mind was calmer, and my balance had improved.

I have been practicing Chi Kung in my own time and with my Sifu for a long time now, and I am grateful for having been awoken to the benefits of this great healing art.

I did not neglect diet. As well as exercising my body and mind in this new way, subtle changes were also made to my diet. I started by introducing natural organic food supplements to my food chain, one of them being Salba, a seed that was eaten by the Aztecs thousands of years ago. It contains ten times more omega 3 than fish oil, and I found it worked wonders for my stiff joints.

I drastically reduced salt intake, and I began to eat less meat. If I did eat meet, it would usually be wild fish or organic chicken. The content of my average dinner plate was now transforming from one of 80% non-organic meat with 20% non-organic greens and vegetables, to one of 80% organic greens and vegetable with 20% organic meat.

Without a doubt, I could feel and see evidence that I was winning the battle with my health challenge. Naturally, I continued to seek out and research natural foods and supplements that I could use to add to my diet.

I once read that today you would have to eat eight to ten oranges to get the same benefit that you would receive from just one orange thirty years ago. In my search I was fortunate enough to come across another great product that would prove to be instrumental in helping me meet my healthy dietary goals.

That product is a green powder that was created by Dr Robert Young, a naturopath and microbiologist. There now exist many different varieties and brands of super green powder. I do not want to mislead today's readers into thinking Dr Young's product is exclusive. I would also suggest you conduct your own research on the benefits of Chlorella and Spirulina.

This green powder is a blend of organic grasses, vegetables, sprouted grains, leaves and high frequency minerals which alkalise, energise, and nourish cells as they balance the body's pH level.

'Super Greens' powder is transformed into a powerful energy drink by adding it to water, and the ingredients within it help to neutralise acid and pull the blood and tissue balance back to its ideal, more alkaline state.

After experimenting with this natural organic product and by fasting on it for seven days, I notice a marked difference in the way my energy levels and muscle power had increased. The feeling was like the feeling I had after practicing Chi Kung, but different. I decided that this organically certified product would become an addition to my food chain, and after many years it still is.

I recalled while sitting in my wheelchair, drinking some homemade fish soup, how I was questioned about my diet. I used the following analogy of a car to explain my mind set:

'If I owned a car, I would never consider putting sand in its fuel tank, so why would I want to put sand in the fuel tank of my body? In other words, fast foods, highly processed foods, foods with high salt and sugar levels, and alcohol. Cigarettes are also poisons that take away health and energy. I don't expect to live forever, but I do expect to have a better quality of life.'

Chlorella and Spirulina in my experience are great products. They are organic and effective super foods, and both chlorella and spirulina are minute plants that grow in fresh water. They are called micro-algae, since they are tiny forms of algae, and they've been around for quite some time: several billion years. These are some of the first and simplest life forms on Earth.

Chlorella is a minute, single-celled, water-grown algae containing a nucleus and an enormous amount of readily available chlorophyll. It also contains approximately 58 percent protein, carbohydrates, all the B vitamins, vitamins C and E, amino acids, and rare trace minerals. In fact, it is virtually a complete food. It contains more vitamin B12 than liver, plus a considerable amount of beta-carotene.

Chlorella and Spirullina have been shown to be effective in treating and even reversing the following conditions:

- Cancers (all types)
- Obesity
- Hypoglycaemia
- Arthritis
- Depression
- Severe liver damage and liver disorders
- Intestinal ulcers
- Haemorrhoids
- Asthma
- High blood pressure
- Constipation
- Bleeding gums
- Infections
- Inflammation of joints and tissues
- Body/breath odour
- Various degenerative diseases
- Essential fatty acid deficiencies
- Mineral deficiencies

I chose to include this profound Cuban experience in this book, not only because I believe that it is relevant, but it is also connected to the bigger picture in a deep and meaningful way.

I'd like to tell you about another uncanny experience that happened roughly a year after my brother's death and whilst I was holidaying in Cuba. In the five plus decades that I have been on this planet, I've been fortunate to have visited different communities around the world, parts of Africa, the Caribbean, USA, and Europe. I have seen that each have a perceived goodness as well as a badness that is unique to that place. Cuba was no exception.

It was against the wishes of certain members of my family and friends and my GP to visit Cuba as it was anticipated that I would suffer an adverse reaction from the sun.

Since my diagnosis, I had been advised to avoid the sun as it could aggravate my condition, but the sun for me was and is life; without the sun everything would stop, including me.

So, I made up my mind to take the opportunity to go on a trip to the island of Cuba with my mother and a close female friend. Whilst I was there, I immersed myself in the sunshine, the music the wildlife and the people. After two and a half weeks, it was now my final afternoon on the island before returning to the UK. I was in 'Old Habana', sitting on a bench outside a touristy shopping complex gazing towards the bluey green sea. My travel companions were buying souvenir stuff in a nearby shop, as I sat outside, reflecting on the great time that I had had and the journey back to the UK.

What I experienced during the hour or so that followed would change the way how I viewed reality and the world. It is something so extremely profound and almost impossible that I was moved beyond words.

I was approached by two men; one was stout and thickly built, wearing baggy jeans and a navy-blue vest. The other guy was tall and slim; he was dressed in all white, from head to toe, a white T shirt, trousers, trainers and baseball cap.

With a strong Latin accent one of these strangers asked, 'You have a light?'

I raised my head and realised they were looking at me, so I politely replied, 'Sorry, I don't smoke.'

'Ah, English,' one of them replied.

Here we go, I thought, expecting to be accosted for money or for them to attempt something worse.

The thickly built man asked me something, I didn't understand so it was unexpectedly translated for me by the man in white. 'He is asking if you would mind if he told you something important?' he said, and added, 'and if I would follow them to their home to meet their wives and children.'

By now my mother and close friend had returned. I briefly explained to them who the two strangers were and what I intended to do. I chose to go, to see where this potentially dangerous encounter would take us. I also felt confident that nothing bad would happen.

The thoughts of being naive and irresponsible raced through my mind but they were soon overcome by a strong sense of calm, confidence and knowing that everything was going to be alright.

My mom gripped my hand nervously, whispering close to my ear, 'They, the two men, are going to kidnap us, rob and kill us.'

I think that the calmness of my voice and the certainty when I told her everything was OK helped to lower my dear mom's blood pressure.

Even though I might have radiated confidence and safety in my thoughts, I wondered if these were indeed conmen plotting our demise. Supposing they were thinking, 'Stupid Englishman.' My mind went into preparedness mode while being cautiously open minded.

'No, I don't mind,' I said, a little too flippantly. 'Let's go.'

I reminded the man dressed in white that our time was limited, and we had to be back at our pick-up point for the hotel minibus as we were flying back home today.

'No problem,' he replied. 'We go not far.'

I may be ignorant, I may be stupid but that voice within was persistently strong and loud, telling me to trust them. So, there I was, trusting them to the point of following them to their home, just five or so minutes away.

We entered the warm sunlit room and were greeted by two smiling ladies who welcomed us with the warmth of the Caribbean sunshine; around five or six young children were standing behind them with eyes wide, looking curiously at us with wonder.

After being introduced to everyone in the home, we sat down and were offered delicious cool drinks of freshly squeezed sugar cane. Then, briefly exiting the room in which we were all seated, the stoutly built man returned and began pointing at me, beckoning me to follow him. I learnt that his name was Babalow.

With an obvious sense of anxiety radiating from my dear mom who was again feeling uneasy, I proceeded to followed Babalow to an adjacent room. She must have had images of the headlines in England the next day, 'English tourist brutally tortured and murdered for cash by man in Cuba.'

Babalow began to say something as he slowly sat down on a dark wooden stool. As he sat, he picked up a rather large leather-covered old book. Babalow beckoned me to sit on a stool opposite him. Immediately he began to utter a string of words; his sentences seemed long and speedy, and the language sounded African with a hint of Spanish. I sat in silence, observing with a kind of hyper-awareness.

Suddenly, unexpectedly Babalow blurted out, 'Your brother is alright, your brother shot.' He pointed to his heart.

If I wasn't already seated, I would have fallen as I was overcome with shock and amazement.

Babalow continued, 'You will be better soon, no more wheelchair, your brother ok.'

I stood up abruptly, my eyes glazed.

'What did you just say?' I asked him to repeat what he had just said.

'Your brother say he is alright and you no more wheelchair, you will be getting better now, no more wheelchair.'

My eyes filled with tears. Here I was on the other side of the world, 5000 miles away, not showing any obvious sings of my health condition and a stranger, who I had just met and who knew nothing about me or my brother, was telling me something that was impossible for him to know. It was like something out of a fantasy film.

At the time, I remember thinking, thinking, and doing more thinking. I was looking for answers. How, why, and what? It seemed like on of those too good to be true stories, a fictional myth. I knew, deep in my soul, it wasn't. Having travelled through such a journey of self-healing from the time of my collapse to being fully fit, I knew enough to know this man I had met in a fleeting moment of stranger meets stranger, that something had happened to connect us. Why else did I follow him back to his home, with my family and all the usual risks?

Reluctantly, I escorted my mom and my partner on a very last-minute trip, using the hotel minibus to buy souvenirs. We had less than five hours left in Cuba and this was a last-minute excursion in a minibus arranged by the hotel to take a handful of tourists into the town to shop.

In the two weeks I spent in Cuba, I travelled from one end of the island to the other and I never met those two men in that time or even discussed my experience of losing my brother with anyone else. Why would I go round telling every stranger a story regarding my brother? Time had moved on a long way from his death and on my break I had been immersed in the beauties of Cuba, the sun, sea, music,and people…Oh, and now and again, the rum.

It was the timing and the randomness of that chance meeting with two complete strangers who had made contact by asking me for a light on my last day, with only a few hours before I had to fly back to the UK, that had hit me with such force.

My face or name had never been in the news, or any media outlet regarding my brother's death, and Facebook was not around back then.

I could not see any way that these two strangers could have found anything out about me and in such a short space of time, without me knowing, and we were practically together 100% of the time.

Back then, getting an internet connection in Cuba was almost impossible, and that was in the hotel. It was even more challenging to find a computer, and one that worked. If it was challenging for tourists to get daily internet or western media news then it would have been virtually impossible for the local people to access world news via the internet. And being a communist country, information and influences from outside western countries was controlled and restricted in Cuba. I doubt that my brother's demise would have made the news in Cuba.

The only thing that these two strangers knew about me during our brief encounter was that my name was Garry, I was from the UK, I didn't smoke, and this was my mom and friend. Nothing more, nothing less, it was as basic as that. We had spent about an hour with them before we were escorted back to our hotel minibus pickup point which I realised was only 10 minutes walking distance from their home.

Going back to the hotel, my brain was still buzzing from the experience. How could this be? I'm over 5000 miles away from home. It is my last day in Cuba, my last few hours. 5000 miles or 5 yards, it makes no diffcrence to those human waves of mind-to-mind connections.

Nevertheless, I was in a communist country where western news and the internet is scarce, I meet two complete strangers, and one of them tells me something about my brother and myself, about which he had no logical way of knowing.

I have always been a healthy sceptic when it came to these matters, and generally I still am, but these guys who I met in Cuba will always be in my heart. Strangers who had a message for me and one that I wasn't deliberately going out looking for. This was the last thing that I expected to experience in my life, much less on my final day on a holiday trip in Cuba. I was astonished, and that moment was special.

'Much of your pain is self-chosen. It is the bitter potion by which the physician within you heals your sick self. Therefore, trust the physician within. And drink his remedy in silence and tranquillity.' Kahlil Gibra.

I found out later that Babalow (my spelling) is spelled Babalaow (West African) and/or Babalao (Caribbean). The name was unfamiliar to me at the time, but I was amazed to find out later that Babalao literally means, 'Father of the mysteries, it is a spiritual name that denotes a high priest.'

Afterword

I have every respect for the medical professionals and appreciate modern physicians and all that they do. In an emergency or with broken limbs they are superb and their knowledge and talents welcome. However, in common with many other specialist individuals, they are very limited when it comes to fixing illnesses of the mind or caused by the mind.

When asked by a specialist why I was refusing medication and I had told them that I felt that it was my body and mind that had put me this way, and that I believed that my body and mind would put me back together again, I also told him that I just needed to be patient while feeding my body wholesome, organic foods, whilst feeding my mind positive, loving and forgiving thoughts. This is not difficult to understand. Yet, they shake their heads and seem to come from a one-dimension and largely negative place. I believe they still have a lot to learn and understand.

When I began to show signs of recovery and was told that this was temporary and that I would relapse after 10 years, it was the same doom mongering, negative response I had grown used to. It's now been about 22 years since that time, and all is well.

I have concluded that the medical system thrives on our sickness. The food we eat and drink, and the negative thoughts, so often generated from watching too much news...and believing it too, make us sick.

When this happens, we go off to see the GP who gives us pills, medicines and injections that are not designed to cure us but to suppress our condition. They afflict us with side effects, and we return to the doctor for more pills, making us more dependent on more drugs which make us more unwell.

I believe that our bodies have all the answers we need, our own personal expert physician. We have just lost our way and have become detached from the knowledge of resilience and self-care.

I don't claim to have the answers but every day, I continue to listen to that voice within me.

It is on this note, that I end my book. After that incident in Cuba, there is nothing much else I can say.

Bibliography

Nothing Lasts Forever-Not Even Your Troubles, Arnold H. Glasgow

Selling Sickness: How the World's Biggest Pharmaceutical Companies Are Turning Us All into Patients, Ray Moynihan and Alan Cassels

The Complete System of Self-Healing Internal Exercise, 1986 Dr Stephen T. Chang

How Your Mind Can Heal Your Body, 2008 David R. Hamilton PhD

The Art of Chi Kung, 1999, Wong Kiew Kit

The Way of Energy, 2005, Master lam

Unlimited Power, 1986, Anthony Robins

Think & Heal Can Your Mind Really Cure Illness, 1999, Professor Kurt Tepperwein

Natural Cure 'They' Don't Want You to Know About, Kevin Trudeau

Healing with Whole Foods, Paul Pitchford

Printed in Great Britain
by Amazon

22318931R00059